Growing Up In Hawaii

By

THOMAS J. MIRANDA

Thomas J Miranda
November 11, 2017

authorHOUSE®

ISBN: 978-1-4107-4576-7 (sc)
ISBN: 978-1-4107-4575-0 (hc)
ISBN: 978-1-4107-4577-4 (e)

This book is printed on acid free paper.

1stBooks – rev. 08/01/03

GROWING UP IN HAWAII
AND OTHER TALES

PREFACE

Growing up can last a lifetime!

This book is a recollection of some significant events in the author's life growing up in Honolulu and experiencing the many challenges of climbing out of a humble beginning and learning to appreciate the value of hard work, trust in God and the importance of family.

After moving to California the author began a whole new experience highlighted in the tales reported herein. My first story, The Lost Sheep, came about when my youngest daughter Julianne asked me to write a story for her. Since I never wrote any stories before, I ducked the request until one day, on a trip to Los Angeles; I decided to write her a story. From that came other stories.

Later, my grandson Nicky who called me Grandpa Bigdog asked me about what I did as a child, so I began writing for him and our other grandchildren, Rebecca, Matthew and Susan.

While working at the Whirlpool Corporation I joined a Bible Group and began writing stories for that group. These are listed in the title Inspirational section.

Finally, I have included some tales and experiences from the business world where I served as a Staff Scientist, Technical Editor and Adjunct Professor.

I am grateful to my wife Carol for her everlasting support and for my mother Olivia who taught us the importance of honesty, the need for prayer and for persistence. She raised five children under very trying conditions, but saw to it that we all succeeded in life. Also my brother Wallance who helped us to get off welfare.

PAUL, THOMAS, LORRAINE, OLIVIA, EVA, WALLANCE MIRANDA

TABLE OF CONTENTS

A REAL HERO

Do you know what a real hero is?

Heroes are people who do extraordinary things in very unusual circumstances. Heroes are made and not born.

Examples of heroes include a kicker who kicks the winning goal in a football game, one who rescues someone from drowning like Uncle Todd did for two ladies who fell into the St. Joseph River or Jesus, who gave us eternal salvation when He died on the cross.

We have a hero in our own family, Uncle Paul.

During World War II, Uncle Paul enlisted in the navy and was assigned to the destroyer USS Hoel, DD533. This Fletcher class destroyer was assigned to a battle group called Taffy 3 in the South Pacific Ocean.

During the invasion of the Philippines this group including the USS Johnston and the USS Samuel B. Roberts were assigned to protect some small aircraft carriers in the Leyte Gulf. One morning on October 25, 1944 they heard some huge splashes in the ocean near the ship. It was the Japanese battleship Kongo and other warships firing from 18 miles away.

These three destroyers headed off to take on the Japanese thinking they were cruisers. The Japanese shells were hitting the Hoel and the shells going right thru the ship, until one hit a reduction gear and stopped the ship in the water. Soon other hits tore the ship apart.

1

Uncle Paul was a loader in the #1 turret of the ship's 5-inch guns when the order came to abandon ship. First Uncle Paul tried to open the hatch, but it would not open, so he ran toward the officer's quarters only to be met by a blazing fire. He ran back to the gun turret and pushed so hard on the dogs holding the hatch shut that he bent them as the ship was sinking by the stern.

(Meanwhile, Great Gramma Bigdog was living on 16 Foote Street in Campbell, California when she heard Uncle Paul calling her at the front door. She ran to the door, but he was not there...he was in the sinking ship).

Uncle Paul was able to push the hatch open and ran to the bow of the ship and jump into the sea as the ship sank stern first. There he found Robert Wilson unconscious floating in the water. Uncle Paul gave him his life jacket just as the Kongo was bearing down on them. He pushed Wilson aside and was struck by the battleship and knocked into the air. After the Kongo passed by, he went to Wilson and dragged him to a life raft and held him in the water for 56 hours until they were rescued.

All three ships had been sunk.

Mr. Wilson lived to become a schoolteacher and Uncle Paul is a Patriot who served his country well and has all the qualifications of a real hero.

AIR RAID SHELTER CURSE

Shortly after the Pearl Harbor Bombing on December 7, 1941, the Hawaiian Islands were subject to martial law. That is, the military had assumed government control and we were to follow rules set out by the military commander. All citizens were issued identification cards and gas masks which we had to carry with us at all times.

One of the requirements laid out by the military was that each household had to dig an air raid shelter. So Uncle Paul, Uncle Wally and Grandpa Bigdog dug an air raid shelter in our front yard at 1822 A Boyd Lane. We dug a large pit, covered it with beams and a tin roof then put dirt on top of the shelter.

Well, when we finished our shelter we went over to Eddie Medeiros' house and helped him dig one. We spent a lot of time digging this big hole in the middle of Eddie's back yard. Johnnie and Walter Mederios also dug with us. In the next yard, Willie Olivera and Stacy Marks were digging a shelter and discovered a skeleton. There was a necklace around the skeleton's neck and Willie and Stacy gathered up the beads and were throwing them around.

In Eddie's yard we too uncovered a skeleton and Walter and Johnnie were throwing the bones around and laughing. Soon it was lunchtime and Uncle Paul and GBD went home. We showed Great Grandma Olivia the necklace beads and she knew that it came from a grave and became very upset with us.

She told us about desecrating a Hawaiian grave and there was a curse which followed those who violated a Hawaiian Grave. People who did that died **a violent death.** Great Grandma Olivia then told us to go back and bury the bones and pray over them.

When we went back, we told them what our mother said, but the kids laughed at us. So Uncle Paul and I gathered up the bones and dug a hole under a mango tree, prayed over the bones and buried them.

Sometime later Stacy Marks was on a navy ship and the ship was sunk. He was trapped inside and died. Willie Olivera had gone on a plane ride and the plane crashed into the ocean.

Many years later Walter Mederios, who had become a successful jockey was killed when his car was struck by a Southern Pacific train in California. Not long after that Johnnie Mederios was riding on the back of a motorcycle when the driver lost control and slammed into a telephone pole, killing Johnnie. Uncle Paul nearly was lost when he was trapped inside the USS Hoel, DD533 that sank of Samar in the South Pacific.

Years later when GBD was a graduate student at Notre Dame, he read an account in the Saturday Evening Post of the curse attached to the disturbing of an Hawaiian grave. After recalling the incidents mentioned above, GBD had a very difficult time sleeping that night and with good reason.

THE BULLY

When Grandpa was a small boy, he lived in Honolulu on Awaiolimu Street. He was too young to attend school, but Uncle Paul and Auntie Eve did go to school. They attended Our Lady of Peace School in downtown Honolulu. To get to school, they used to walk down Awaiolimu street to Lusitana street and then down Emma street to Fort Street where the church and school were.

Just down the street from our house, three doors down, lived a bully named Gilbert Peterson. He used to pick on us every chance he had and made life miserable for us.

One day as Uncle Paul and Auntie Eve were walking home from school, they got just three houses from home, when Gilbert the Bully jumped out from behind a stone wall and would not let them pass.

What do you think they could do?

Well, Uncle Paul put his books down and told Auntie Eve to wait there. He then walked all the way down Awaiolimu street, down Lusitana street and to Emma street (don't you have a friend named Emma, Nicky?) where there was a Japanese school yard. In the schoolyard were a group of bamboo bushes. Uncle Paul had a pocket knife with him, so he cut a long branch, about four feet long and headed back to where Gilbert the Bully was holding Auntie Eve hostage.

The bully laughed at Uncle Paul until he saw the bamboo switch in his hand. Uncle Paul then proceeded to whip his legs with the switch and chased him up the street and into his yard, yelling and screaming.

After that day, the bully never bothered Uncle Paul and Auntie Eve ever again.

ANOTHER BULLY

When Grandpa Bigdog was a little boy, we moved from Auwaiolimu Street to 1822 A Boyd Lane. At the end of this lane lived another bully named George Costa. He always gave Uncle Paul and I a hard time and we did not like him.

One day Uncle Paul and I found a small steering wheel and decided to make a skate car with a hood on the front. Uncle Paul built the car and I told him that I knew how to hook up the steering wheel, which was not true. So when the car was finished, Grandpa nailed the ropes that steered the skate car to a broom handle. At the end of the handle, we attached the steering wheel...the skate car was complete and ready for a test ride.

We took the car up to Lusitana Street and Uncle Paul sat on the seat and I pushed him down the sidewalk. As we went down the walk, the skate car drifted off toward the right and Uncle Paul turned the steering wheel to the left and the skate car ran off the sidewalk into a fence. Grandpa had connected the steering ropes backwards so that when we turned the wheel to go left, the car went right and when we turned it to the right the car turned left.

After a little practice we got the hang of it and remembered that all the steering had to be done backward, but we managed to enjoy the new skate car.

ENTER THE BULLY!

As we were enjoying our new skate car along came George Costa, the bully down Boyd Lane. (Remember the story of the other bully, Gilbert Peterson and how Uncle Paul took care of him?) He demanded that we let him ride our new skate car and pushed Uncle Paul off the car.

4

We were close to Kuakini Street that was a steep hill with a big stonewall along one side. We led him to the top of the hill and as he got on we gave him a big push and he roared down the street. As he sailed down the skate car began to drift to the right and he jerked the steering wheel to the left only to crash into the stonewall. He went tumbling down the sidewalk and never bothered us again.

BEE WARE

When Uncle Paul and I were little boys, we moved to 1822 A Boyd Lane in Honolulu. This was close to our previous home on Auwaiolimu Street, but to us it was a long ways off. In Hawaii there are many beautiful flowers, one of which is the hibiscus. You should have Daddy find you a picture of a hibiscus flower.

Near our house was a big hedge of hibiscus and when it was in bloom it was very beautiful with many colors. The honeybees loved to get nectar from these flowers and if you listened, you could hear them buzzing from flower to flower as they crawled into the flower to reach the nectar at the bottom of the blossom.

One day Uncle Paul decided to play a trick on the honeybee. As the bee crawled to the bottom of the flower, he reached behind the flower and closed it, trapping the bee inside the blossom. In this way he was able to catch the bee. So he carried that blossom around to show it to Grandpa and Auntie Lorraine. After awhile he went back and got another one, but this time he squeezed the flower too hard and the bee stung him on the finger. Uncle Paul dropped the flower and ran home to put Rawleigh's ointment on the bee sting.

In another bee affair Uncle Paul was the star of the show. In Kailua, Auntie Annie had a big yard and kept cows, chickens, ducks and pigs. To keep the cows in Uncle Joe (we called him Double Rope) made a barbed wire fence. The fence posts were made from ironwood, a hard pinewood that grows in Hawaii. Bumblebees used to bore holes in the posts and we would try to catch them by plugging the holes, putting a glass jar on one hole and tapping the post with a stick. As the bumblebees came out they flew into jar. One day Uncle Paul was trapping bumble bees but he forgot to cover all the holes and the bumblebees came flying out and chased him through the coconut trees.

So…when it comes to playing with bees don't forget to **BEEWARE!**

BEWARE OF BOOGO

When Grandpa Bigdog was a little boy, he lived in Honolulu on the slopes of a volcanic crater called Punchbowl, because it looked like a big punch bowl. Near Grandpa's house lived an old Hawaiian man. The older kids called him "Boogo"

Boogo used to plant sweet potatoes in his garden and we usually saw him walking around the yard carrying a gunny sack with potatoes in the sack. The older kids used to tease Uncle Paul and I by telling us that Boogo was going to catch us and put us in the gunnysack.

When we used to walk up Puuwaina Drive to go to the top of Punchbowl, we had to pass Boogo's house, so we always crossed the street and walked as far away from his house as possible until we got past his house. We were so afraid that he would come after us with his gunnysack!

One day Grandpa Bigdog got sick and Great Grandma, Olivia, had to take him to Palama Settlement. Since we were on welfare, we could not afford to go to a doctor, so we went to Palama to get medical help. So we walked down Awaiolimu Street to where the streetcar was on Lusitana Street. The tracks ended there and they would change the wire to make the streetcar go the other way back to Honolulu.

As we were standing there, guess who showed up to ride the streetcar?

BOOGO!!

Grandpa Bigdog was so scared he thought Boogo would grab me. I hung onto Great Grandma until we got to Palama Settlement. What a scary ride that was...so Nicky, watch out for **BOOGO!**

BROTHER LEO

When Grandpa Bigdog was in grade school, GBD attended Cathedral School on Nuuanu Avenue. Cathedral School was run by the Marian Brothers and was associated with Our Lady of Peace Church in Honolulu.

The Principal was Brother Eugene Merkel who also taught 8th grade. Brother Leonard taught 7th grade and Brother Leo Mulrey taught 5th grade. Brother Leo was a real tyrant who ran roughshod over us boys and made sure we were kept in line.

Attending this school were Uncle Paul, Uncle Wally and GBD. Some of my friends who also attended were Johnnie, Eddie and Walter Medeiros. Other inmates at the school included Paul Magnani, another good friend of GBD, Stanley Machado, who Johnnie called Mashode, Willie Olivera and Watson Shun.

Cathedral School was next door to the Japanese Embassy and they had a very nice garden. We used to watch big black Packard cars drive in with Japanese dignitaries arriving and leaving.

One of the problems teaching a gang like us was that the brothers were strict disciplinarians. That is you never got away with anything.

Eddie Medeiros used to sit in Brother Leo's class and pass notes and make funny faces at him and we thought this was fun, but Brother Leo had other ideas. So when Brother Leo was writing at the blackboard, Eddie and I used to start acting up since he had his back turned to us, he didn't know what we were up to.

Well, lo and behold, out of nowhere came an eraser flying out of Brother Leo's hand and conked either Eddie or GBD on the head. What

Eddie and I didn't know was that Brother Leo could see through his glasses the reflection of us horsing around and could throw an eraser faster than we could say "DUCK".

Brother Leo also had it in for Uncle Paul. He would take great pleasure of writing a big F on Uncle Paul's homework papers and make fun of Uncle Paul...something we all did not appreciate.

I'll bet if Brother Leo could see Uncle Paul, Eddie and GBD now, he wouldn't think we were so dumb.

Nicky, if you look at the picture the man on the left is Eddie and on the right is Uncle Paul. The reason they look a little older is that after being in Brother Leo's class, you too would look old.

BROWN SLACKS

When Grandpa Bigdog went to college he attended San Jose State College. GBD worked nights in the Sunnyvale Theater as a movie projectionist and usually did not get enough sleep.

GBD made it through the first quarter and started the second quarter in January. Aunt Lorraine also went to San Jose State and one day she told GBD that he looked like a bum wearing blue jeans and a plaid shirt.

So GBD decided to go all out and get a new wardrobe. He went to Sears and told the clerk that he wanted a pair of slacks, "Price is no object...I want the cheapest slacks you have", said GBD. The clerk showed GBD a pair of brown woolen slacks for the huge sum of $4.85. So GBD went home with a new pair of slacks and would be the hit of the campus.

One of the classes GBD took was Chemistry 1B and he never read the laboratory manual before class. What GBD would do is go to class and read the manual like a cookbook.

GBD's lab partner was Tom Lauret who was an Entomology Major and he too came to class unprepared.

So the first day that GBD wore his expensive brown slacks to class, to show it off to Tom who in turn, showed GBD his new sport shirt that his Aunt gave him. It was a pretty shirt, white with green flowers.

So off we went to do our experiments. Today we were supposed to fill a number of test tubes with 5-10 ml of liquids and heat...then observe. For example if we heated the liquid over a burner and it bubbled, we were to write in the notebook the result of the experiment.

One of the problems with doing this is that the liquids could superheat and shoot out of the test tube.

Sure enough Tom was heating something and it shot out of the test tube all over the front of GBD's new slacks.

"What was that? ", I asked.

"I don't know", was his reply.

Soon GBD was heating something and it too shot out of the test tube all over Tom Lauret's shirt.

"What was that? ", He asked.

"I don't know", was my reply.

Well, we soon tired of chemistry and decided to go to the Huddle to get some coffee. It was a beautiful sunny day in February and we were glad to get out of the lab. After drinking our coffee and complaining about a thousand things we headed back to the lab.

As we walked out in the sun, Tom's shirt began to turn black and he was furious. I had sprayed him with silver nitrate and it was developing in the sunlight. I told him that he too had shot me with a liquid, but he countered that nothing happened to my slacks and he was correct.

Two weeks later, I was wearing my brown slacks and I walked over to the library where Tom, Frank Passantino, Matt Krumpotic and Don Mertens were standing. I put down my books and put my hands into my pockets and the whole front of my pants disintegrated, leaving me standing in my underwear.

You see, Tom had squirted GBD with concentrated sulfuric acid and it denatured the wool in my slacks. The only good thing that came out of this is that GBD uses this story in his Polymer Chemistry class at Indiana University to illustrate polymer degradation.

Well, back to blue jeans!

CLOSE ELECTION

When Grandpa Bigdog first came to California from Honolulu, he was quite confused since the culture from which he came was so much different from that in California. He never thought he could ever assimilate with that crowd since many of the students had grown up in Campbell.

Campbell was a small town surrounded by prune and apricot orchards, the principal crops supporting the economy there.

At Campbell High School GBD noted that some of the popular students became members of the Student Council, the top job being the Student Body

President. GBD used to daydream about being able to someday get elected to the student council, but that was a very remote dream.

Well, when GBD was a junior, he was elected to the student council and the next great step was to be the Student Body President.

One of the important students at Campbell High was Paul Meyer. He was a very serious individual and excelled in everything he attempted. When he was a student in Cambrian Grammar School, he and his good friend Ray Flagg made a pact that when they got to high school, Paul would run for Student Body President and Ray would be his campaign manager.

Ray Flagg was also a very good friend of GBD and a talented artist. Ray was also creative and would be a formidable force in any campaign for election. So when election time came up, Ray apologized for not supporting me explaining his pact with Paul.

So, GBD had to find another campaign manager. Larry Lewis turned out to be a good manager, who was also artistic. We also enlisted the talents of Emily Von Gunden to do the artwork.

Ray set out to create attractive signs that he put on the bulletin boards and around the school grounds. We heard that the day before the election, Ray and Paul were planning a big surprise. So GBD had to come up with something to counter their big offensive.

GBD asked Larry Lewis' mother to sew a flag made from an old flour sack with the word TOM on each side of the flag. Then Uncle Paul made a flagpole with a pulley at the top and cords to raise the flag.

GBD played saxophone in the school band so he got the band organized to do a march on the day of the big surprise.

Well, behind the school building was a large parking area where the busses unloaded the students. This was where Uncle Paul mounted the flagpole.

What were Ray Flagg and Paul Meyer up to? That was the big question. Well, we found out the next day.

Ray had painted the words **PAUL MEYER FOR PRESIDENT** on a large roll of paper and stretched it across the lawn behind the library so that the students getting off the bus could see this huge sign.

Well, GBD borrowed a 1910 Dodge Touring Sedan from David Keesling who parked it in front of the school. During lunch hour GBD, then had the band march around the main building parading a sign reading TOM. As the band marched around David Keesling drove the sedan with Mac Martin; Larry Lewis and GBD sat in the back. David then drove into the area where the busses parked and Larry Lewis and Mac Martin got out and raised the flag as the band played. The whole student body watched with their backs to Ray's big sign. Then GBD gave a speech, got back into the car and drove off.

The next day the elections results were in: Paul Meyer 85, Tom Miranda 512.

Years later Paul started Success Motivation and was its Chairman. He became a very successful businessman and a great Christian.

GBD IN FRONT OF CAMPBELL HIGH SCHOOL

1-2-4-3

When Grandpa Bigdog lived in Campbell, California, he bought a 1927 Model T from Mervin Nelson for the huge sum of $5.00. This was a black coupe and it had no muffler, meaning that it could be heard around the whole town of Campbell.

Now this car did not run everyday, so when I was lucky enough to start it, I would drive around town and pick up Mac Martin or Ray Flagg and cruise around making a lot of noise and having fun. This car was fun to drive and must have had a lot of history to it.

Soon GBD noted that other friends began to buy Model T's and drive them around town. Rex Jeffers bought a model T from Manuel (Pickineen) Miranda, our cousin, who owned an orchard on East Campbell Avenue.

One day Rex challenged GBD to a race. So we took off down Foote Street and up Hawthorne back to Campbell Avenue then back to Foote Street. Rex won the race easily. But, GBD noticed that one of the spark plug wires had come off his car. So GBD replaced the wire and challenged Rex to another race. This time GBD won easily and Rex decided that he had to make some repairs to his car.

GBD noticed a knock in the engine and decided to take the engine apart. There were quite a few bolts around the bottom pan of the engine, but eventually GBD got the pan off so he could see the connecting rods. Well two of the connecting rods were held on by only one bolt, the other having come off. No wonder the engine was knocking and it is a wonder that GBD did not throw a rod through the block. So after finding the necessary bolts and replacing the pan, GBD started up the engine. Well, you cannot imagine how much more power the engine had with all cylinders now properly connected to the crankshaft.

GBD's good friend Ray Flagg also bought a Model T, but it was not in running condition. So GBD went over to Ray's house on Apricot Avenue to help Ray get his car running. Well Ray had disconnected the ignition coils and the ignition wires. So we set out to fix the engine. Well, the Model T has four electrical coils, which produce 25,000 volts of electricity to fire the spark plugs. The wires from the coils go the distributor to fire a sparkplug when the piston reaches the top of the compression stroke.

So here is the mess Ray and I had. We were like the 'blind leading the blind' since we did not know the firing order of each cylinder. So GBD came up with an idea. He removed all of the spark plugs and had Ray crank the engine, while GBD put his finger over the sparkplug hole to see which cylinder had compression. When we got compression on the first cylinder we then connected the sparkplug wire to the first coil.

Now, what is the next step?

Well, GBD then figured that the firing order would be 1-4-2-3 so we attached the wires accordingly and began to crank the engine. To start a Model T one had to have the brake all the way on to push the transmission into neutral, then pull on the choke and hope for the best. Cranking a Model T is not much fun, and you had to be aware of backfire where the crank would snap backward and break a wrist.

When we got set we started cranking and the engine fired, sputtered and stalled. We were encouraged with this and cranked till we were exhausted. After awhile we abandoned this approach and tried other combinations. Each time we got some firing, but the engine never ran. We continued on this mission for a number of evenings with no avail.

One day a friend of Ray who was an auto mechanic came by and told us that we had the wrong combination. The correct combination was 1-2-4-3. We reconnected the wires in this configuration and lo and behold the car started and ran. Ray and I were delighted and soon Ray was riding around Campbell in his own Model T.

COCONUTS

Grandpa Bigdog lived in Honolulu and spent most of his growing up in the city. Since we were on welfare and it was the depression, there was little money available. One big luxury was at Christmas time when Great Grandma Olivia bought a whole case of soda water, all flavors, and we thought we had gone to heaven, being able to drink a whole bottle of soda water.

Auntie Annie and Uncle Joe (Double Rope) lived on the other side of the island. Their children were Peter, Elsie, Albert, William (Sonny), Nina, and Walter. Double Rope was a dairy farmer and he had a dairy in Waimanalo, next to Julian Jama's dairy and near the Girls School. I remember the house stood out on a hillock and they had a big REO Speed Wagon next to the milk room.

Double Rope then bought a home in Kailua, a big blue house on an acre of property. The house was situated in the middle of a large coconut grove that stretched from Lanikai to Mokapu Point. Near Kailua Bay there was a long stand of ironwood trees that acted as a windbreak.

Coconut trees were everywhere and we used to climb the trees to knock green coconuts down and eat them. At night the wind blew thru the coconut trees and made a very peaceful sound that I can remember to this day.

The whole area around Kailua was strewn with fallen coconut branches and fallen coconuts. As the coconuts ripened they would fall to the ground.

Enter Mr. Costa!

Mr. Costa used to buy coconuts and sell them to a distributor. In order to sell a coconut to him, it would have to be properly ripened. We tested this by shaking the coconut to hear the water splash inside. This would indicate that the coconut would be marketable.

Now, I mentioned that we had a little money and no real way to earn money, but coconuts were our roads to fortune. You see Mr. Costa would pay us a penny for each coconut.

So everyday Uncle Paul, Sonny, and GBD would go through the coconut grove looking for fallen coconuts like we were hunting for treasure. We each had a gunnysack in which to put our coconuts. We would then take them to Auntie Annie's yard and place them in a pile.

I had a pile under a coconut tree, under the next coconut tree was Uncle Paul's and further on was Sonny's pile of treasure. Everyday we would count our coconuts. Sonny had the most coconuts since he was a skilled hunter. I had accumulated 18 coconuts and just couldn't imagine what I was going to do with all that money.

On an appointed day, Auntie Annie told us that Mr. Costa was coming for the coconuts. We all ran out and recounted our coconuts, being careful that no one had snitched our coconuts.

Here comes Mr. Costa! He got out of his truck and began to count and shake coconuts making sure he could hear the coconut water splash around inside. [He had been known to discard coconuts costing us big money.]

Well, he finished his job, loaded his truck and said Aloha until next time. We sat around counting our money the rest of the day, remembering that tomorrow we would have to go out to find coconuts for his next visit.

ELSIE, MYRTLE (NINA), SONNY, WALTER AND PETER CARVALHO

DEMONSTRATION

When Grandpa Bigdog was in college he was required to take a course on Student Teaching. This class did not meet regularly on campus, but involved GBD to go to a school and spend the day observing and eventually teaching a class for a six week period.

One of the tasks which student teachers were urged to do was to motivate the students and to encourage their attention concerning the subject material. Education professors told us to use demonstrations and especially impressive ones to keep student attention.

Being a chemistry teacher, it was fairly easy to make demonstrations because of all the avenues available using color changes, electrical or magnetic demonstrations. Remember when GBD did the Tesla coil and Jacob's ladder at Los Gatos High School? [See Student Teacher]

Well another student teacher that learned about impressing the students decided to do a spectacular demonstration and in fact, this too happened at Los Gatos High School, but before GBD had taught there.

There is a chemical process called Thermit used to repair broken railroad tracks or large metal shafts like ship propeller shafts. Thermit is a mixture of aluminum powder and iron oxide. The two powders are mixed and placed into a mold over the broken track. To ignite the Thermit mixture one must light a strip of magnesium metal and plunge it into the mixture. There after there is a big blast of smoke and the ensuing reaction produces molten iron, which melts at 1545 ° centigrade. The molten iron repairs the broken rail or shaft.

One day an eager student teacher decided he would make a demonstration of thermit to his class. So he filled a 600 ml beaker with a mixture of iron oxide and aluminum powder and lit it with a magnesium ribbon. The reaction took off like a $7 shotgun and sparks flew all over the place. The students were shouting ooh's and aaah's as the reaction proceeded. The student was pleased that he had gotten the students attention.

But what he didn't realize was that he had overplayed his luck. The molten iron melted its way through the bottom of the beaker, the desktop, the floor and down onto a table in the library below.

The students will never forget that demonstration for a long time.

Grandpa Bigdog never learned if that student teacher ever got a job teaching in high school.

STUDENT TEACHER

When Grandpa Bigdog was in college he was studying to be a High School Science Teacher. One of the most demanding and dreaded courses in student teaching was Curriculum a 5 unit course and the bane of all prospective teachers. The course work involved preparing numerous papers, source material, motivational tools, lesson plans and a host of busybody projects. Lucky for GBD, he was able to take the course in the summer and avoided all the nonsense taught in the regular sessions at San Jose State College.

When GBD got to student teaching, he was sent to Los Gatos High School and taught chemistry and advanced algebra. Student teaching involved sitting in the class and observing the resident teacher and assisting the teacher when needed.

After a few weeks, we got to the end of a unit in chemistry and the next unit was to be Atomic Theory. So on a Friday afternoon the teacher told me to take over the class on Monday and teach this class for six weeks.

Grandpa Bigdog worked his way through college by running movies at the Sunnyvale Theater. Each night the theater manager gave GBD a schedule on a piece of paper the size of a half sheet of regular paper. This information told GBD which movies to run and what time each would start.

Late Sunday night GBD realized that he would have to start thinking about the next six weeks, so he took the schedule sheet and on the back side divided it into four sections and outlined what he wanted to cover: History, Subatomic particles, Tools for nuclear processes and People.

After the movie closed GBD drove to San Jose State and picked up some magnets, cathode ray tubes and other gadgets. GBD also had built a Tesla coil and he gathered that into a box and was ready for school.

On Monday morning as GBD was walking into school, Dr. Rich of the Education Department greeted me at the door and told me he was going to sit in on my first class. I took my supplies into the lab and waited for the class to begin. Dr. Rich asked to see my syllabus and outline for the next six weeks and I showed him my theater schedule and he nearly threw up!

He flew into a fit of rage and demanded how I could possibly teach for six weeks on only a sheet of paper.

"This I must see", he said looking very angry.

When class started I divided the class into four groups to cover each topic I outlined then gave them a real dog and pony show with huge sparks flying, bending electron beams with magnets and showing Jacob's ladder.

The students were thrilled and got to work on their projects with enthusiasm. The resident teacher was very pleased and amazed…and so was Dr. Rich.

After that day Grandpa Bigdog became the talk of the Education Department and Dr. Rich said he had never seen such a performance from a student teacher.

CRICKETS

When Grandpa Bigdog lived in California, he had a very good friend Kent Clark. Kent's father owned the Clark's Drug Store in Campbell and he and I spent a lot of time talking about many subjects. Kent's brother Dan was a physician and Kent had some trouble figuring what he wanted to do when he grew up. This same thing can be said of GBD who also is still trying to figure out what to do when he grows up.

Kent took a lot of turns into various fields. For a while he was interested in astronomy, then microbiology, then thought about getting a teaching job at a university. He also got interested in geology and later became a Paleontologist with the Shell Oil Company in Houston, Texas from which he recently retired.

While he was getting into geology, he expressed some interest in volcanology. GBD was also interested in volcanoes since he lived on the slopes of one in Honolulu. So one Saturday afternoon, Kent came by the house and told me that he was going to visit Mono Craters near Yosemite National Park.

So GBD threw a sleeping bag in his car and off we went to Reno, Nevada. We stayed overnight there and the next morning headed out for the Mono Craters area to the south. Well, we got to the valley below the craters and it was quite hot. As far as the eye could see were acres of sagebrush and desert sand. So we began our trek toward the base of the craters.

Since it got hotter, Kent decided to turn back and do some target shooting. GBD told Kent that he wanted to climb Mono Crater and proceeded along the desert floor. As he walked along, there were a lot of crickets making noise. It seemed that with each step, another cricket would make a noise. This went on until GBD reached a saddle between two craters and he started up to the top of Mono Crater.

After almost two hours, GBD reached the top of the crater. What a splendid view of the craters and the surrounding valley. GBD was tired so he sat down to enjoy the view. While sitting there, GBD remembered Uncle Paul, who loved to hunt, telling him about rattlesnakes in the desert and woods.

"Those were not crickets, they were rattlesnakes!!"

GBG came flying down the mountain and in a few minutes had reached the bottom of the crater near the saddle between the craters. Then came the long trek back across the desert floor. Each step GBD took evoked a rattle and GBD would turn completely around to see if there were any snakes around. Finally, GBD reached Kent's car and urged him to get out of there as fast as possible.

Crickets?

GBD IN FRONT OF THE CAMPBELL THEATER

DIRTY MOVIE

When Grandpa Bigdog was in college he worked his way through as a movie projectionist. His first job was in the Campbell Theater when he was in high school. GBD used to run the movies and got $4.00 a night for his work. This was a good source of income and it lasted until GBD graduated from school.

After graduation GBD worked as an electrician in Drew's cannery and still kept his job in the Campbell Theater.

After starting college, the projectionists formed a union and GBD became a member of the IATSE Local 796. The Campbell Theater job went to another man, so GBD was sent to the Cinema, a theater in Mt. View showing Mexican films. Later, he moved to the Sunnyvale Theater until he graduated.

After graduation, GBD started teaching at San Jose State College. The attitude toward bad behavior was much stricter in those days and if any faculty member was caught doing something bad, he was fired.

Since teaching was a full time job, GBD quit the Sunnyvale Theater and became what is known as a relief operator, that is GBD would go to different theaters one night a week to run movies so the regular operator (projectionist) could have the night off.

As a result GBD ran movies in the Campbell, Los Gatos, Mt. View, Sunnyvale and Cinema theaters on different nights. The Campbell Theater had developed a different schedule. They would close on Wednesday nights and other programs would be added to use up the vacancy.

One Wednesday night they announced that they were going to show a dirty movie. This was a movie filming of the San Diego Burlesque show and a far cry from the trash they now label "Dirty Movies".

The business agent for our union was Jack Sandgren, who called GBD up and told him to run the dirty movie next Wednesday.

So next Wednesday after coming home from a long day at San Jose State College, GBD was eating supper when he noticed Jack walking toward our home on Foote Street.

"Why don't you go to Sunnyvale tonight and I'll run the dirty movie", he said. So GBD got into his old 1934 Ford and drove to Sunnyvale. (Remember the 3 Gallon story?)

The next morning the headline in the San Jose Mercury News read:

CAMPBELL THEATER RAIDED; PROJECTIONIST ARRESTED

There was a big picture of Jack Sandgren on the front page.
This became the talk of the town!
Lucky for GBD that Jack had decided to send me to Sunnyvale or my teaching career would have been short lived.

DREAM COME TRUE

When Granpa Bigdog was in high school, he had some very good friends. These include Mac Martin, Kent Clark, Larry Lewis, Ray Flagg and Merrill Grim. Merrill's father was the Postmaster in Campbell.

Merrill had attended Santa Clara University while GBD was a student at San Jose State College. One day GBD was standing at the railroad crossing in Campbell when the crossing signal began to wigwag. So GBD waited for the train to come past. But as the train was nearing the crossing it slowed down and stopped. That was when Merrill, carrying his books climbed down from the engine.

19

Merrill has hitch hiked from Santa Clara and got a ride as far as Bascome Avenue, then decided to take a shortcut by walking along the railroad tracks. As he was walking along, the train stopped and the engineer asked Merrill is he needed a ride, so he came home by train that day.

Merrill later entered the Marine Corps and was sent to Korea. GBD used to write him and one day in April GBD got a letter from him telling GBD that he was going to be discharged in June and that maybe he and I could go camping in the Trinity Mountains.

A few days later GBD had a strange dream. He dreamed about climbing a mountain with Merrill. The mountain was very high and it seemed that GBD would never reach to top. Merrill had gotten ahead of GBD and reached the edge of a cliff and waited for GBD to catch up to him.

Well, at that point Merrill said that the trail ended and we couldn't go any higher. From the edge of the cliff and to the right was a high mountain with two lakes. Suddenly, GBD turned right into some manzanita bushes and found a trail and proceeded down the trail to a small valley. Right across the trail was a huge ponderosa pine tree that had fallen over the trail and GBD remembered looking up at the roots of the tree high in the air. Here GBD woke up.

In August, Merrill came home from Korea and one day he came by with some geological service maps of the Trinity Mountain area and showed GBD where he wanted to go camping. So we planned a trip and got our supplies ready. GBD had a small black dog Jose and since I had no one to watch him, we decided to take him along. So we fixed a harness with a few cans of dog food for him. So on the appointed day we left Campbell and headed up for the Trinity Mountains area. We found a cabin to spend the night and the next day set up to the high mountains where there were two lakes, according to the map.

We began our trek up the mountain. It was a tough climb and being out of shape GBD had a tough time climbing the mountain. On our way up, Jose startled a porcupine and chased him up a tree. As we continued to climb the mountain got steeper and it seemed that we could never make it to the top.

Well, Merrill was ahead of me and he called back to tell me that we had lost the trail. GBD finally caught up and stood at the edge of a cliff where the trail ended. To our right we saw a high mountain and two lakes. GBD suddenly turned and told Merrill to follow and he walked through some manzanita bushes and found a trail. This was great as the trail led down to a small valley. As we went along there was a large ponderosa pine tree laying across the trail. As GBD went by the stump he remembered the dream and the hair on the back of his neck stood up.

I had been there before!!

MAC MARTIN MERRILL GRIM GRANDPA BIGDOG

FDR DIED TODAY

Historical facts are sometimes lost from the memory, but the day that President Franklin D. Roosevelt died, April 12, 1945 will always stick in Grandpa Bigdog's memory. Why?

Well on that date I was on my way to a track meet at Lincoln High School in San Jose with a lot of my friends on the track team. These included Mac Martin, Merrill Grim, Frutie (Richard Villafuerte), Jerry Finch, Bob Hall and Tommy Blackmun. The reason I was on the team was that I ran the mile. Lincoln High was a big rival of Campbell High and we were somewhat outnumbered in many areas.

As we were sitting in the locker room waiting for the meet to begin, the coach Walter Hill came in and told us that President Roosevelt died. This had a quieting effect on everyone. Then came for me another shocker. Coach Hill told me that he wanted me to run the half-mile instead since we were short of runners. Merrill Grim would run the mile.

Well, I had never run the half-mile in competition before and did not really know how to run a pace or just what to do. So, I got up to the starting line realizing that I needed to run two laps around the track (880 yards) for this event.

The gun sounded and about eight of us roared down the track. One big guy got into the lead so I decided to follow him and I matched him step for step. As we rounded the turn and came to the back track, I could hear a lot of shouting from the crowd. Soon I was finishing the first lap right behind the big guy as the timekeeper called out: 56, 57, 58 seconds. I had covered the first lap in 55 seconds, faster then I ever did.

"Wow!, Wow!" came from the grand stand as we rounded the second turn. Then as I got to the backstretch I suddenly felt that someone had dropped a 50 pound sack of potatoes on my back. I had run out of gas. My legs got heavier as I struggled on. Soon all the runners zoomed past me and I came in last.

What I did not know was that the big guy in front of me was Dick Bartholomew, the California State Champion half-miler. The reason for all the audience cheering was that in the first lab they could not believe someone could challenge him and of course I sure could not.

I should have known it was going to be a bad day when I had heard FDR died, so did this track star.

Frutie and Grandpa Bigdog

FIGHTER PLANES

When Grandpa Bigdog was living in Honolulu, there were many by military bases on the island. There were many Forts and two naval bases, Pearl Harbor and Kaneohe Naval Airbase on the Kailua side of Oahu.

We used to watch the big PBY Catalina flying boats flying back to Pearl Harbor near sunset each day. These large airplanes would fan out each morning at 5 a.m. and return at 5 p.m. They would scout the ocean for enemy ships. There were also many smaller airplanes. One of our favorites was the Curtiss P-40 fighter. This was a sleek airplane and it was fast.

What was so interesting about this is that when Pearl Harbor was attacked on December 7, 1941, the Catalina flying boats did not go out that morning. President Roosevelt told General Short that they could only fly to the southwest. (The Japanese fleet was located in the northwest and had the Catalinas gone out as usual they would have found the Japanese fleet.)

The people in Hawaii all knew that a war was brewing with Japan, it was only a matter of time.

GBD used to love watching navy ships come in to Pearl Harbor. Usually, when the fleet came back to base the aircraft carriers would anchor off Waikiki Beach and it was a sight to behold. I can remember seeing the USS Lexington and USS Yorktown sitting off shore.

Uncle Paul and GBD had a weekend job near Mokapu Point. A group of Honolulu businessmen had a skeet club on Kapoho Point and we used to crank the skeet traps. For this we were paid $2.50, big money for us.

GBD remembers the last time we cranked traps was on December 6, 1941. When we finished our work, two of the businessmen gave us a ride as far as Kaimuki and we took a bus home.

The next morning GBD went to 7:00 a.m. mass and got home at 7:40. GBD then went down Boyd lane to a small park. As I walked across the park GBD heard a whistle as a shell flew overhead and exploded on the slopes of Punchbowl. Soon several more shells came flying and we kids decided that the military were having maneuvers.

So we looked over at Pearl Harbor and saw a lot of airplanes diving down and huge clouds of black smoke rising. We could see planes diving down the turning up after dropping bombs or torpedoes. Some planes crashed. We watched this from about 8 a.m. on.

As we were standing there we heard fighter planes above with machine guns blazing. All of a sudden a Japanese plane came right over us, about 100 feet in the air. We could see the rising sun on the wing tips and a big sun on the tail. The pilot was working the control stick for all he was worth; as he was being chased by two P40 fighters with their machine guns blazing. We watched this until they disappeared from view.

After a while, Uncle Paul found GBD in the park and told me there was a war going on. We ran home.

About 10:00 a.m. Uncle Paul, GBD and Aunts Eva and Lorraine were standing out on Lusitana Street when we heard a screaming shell coming. We dived behind a stone wall as the shell exploded spraying the wall with hot shrapnel. Uncle Paul picked up a piece and it burnt his hand. Aunt Eve still has that piece of shrapnel.

After that we really go worried. The food stores were closed and martial law was declared. Anyone caught looting would be shot. At night there was a complete blackout. It was strange to look out at night and not see a single light burning.

Nihau, one of the islands, was captured by the Japanese. The pilot got lost and landed there. He rounded up the villagers and took over the island. After a while he got into an argument with a Hawaiian man. The Japanese pilot shot the man in the abdomen and made him mad. He picked up the pilot and smashed him to the ground, then got into a boat and rowed to Kauai for help.

The next September, GBD and the family got on the USS Mt. Vernon, a troop ship and sailed off to California. Uncle Wally who worked at Pearl Harbor remained behind and supported the family.

P40 FIGHTER PLANE

FREE CANDY

When Grandpa Bigdog lived in Honolulu we lived on the slopes of Punchbowl. This is a large volcanic crater situated right in the center of the city. One of the values of this was all the steep hills which made for great skating, bike riding and for running skate cars.

Near our home on Boyd lane was a grocery store run by two Chinese men and it was called CHIN HO LEE store. One of the attractions was a large case in the front of the store that contained candy. Now candy to us was such items as cracked seed, sweet and sour semoi (dried plum) mango seed, preserved olives that we called footballs because of the shape, ginger and sawa (sour)seed, a very salty form of dried plum. All of these were stored in large glass jars sitting on top of the candy counter and some inside the counter. These were mouthwatering treats unavailable to us, since we had no money to buy them.

Rich kids like Maddie and Kekaa Boyd (rich because they could afford to buy a sack of semoi) were the envy of Uncle Paul and I. What was real torture was to stand in front of those candy jars and drool. Once in a while we could come up with a nickel and were able to buy a sack of semoi. This was a real treasure and we relished that treat.

One of the facts we knew living in Hawaii was that we were going to have a war with Japan and the natives there had no doubt that it would happen. Also we used to have practice blackout drills to test our ability to darken the island in case of an air raid.

Now, because of this impending disaster, it was easy to dream up a solution to getting some free candy. Uncle Paul, Eddie Medeiros and GBD used to talk about this all the time. We figured that if there was a war, the Japanese would bomb the store and we could then pick up free semoi. This was not a bad idea in that kid thinking is not very rational.

So along came December 7, 1941 and the bombs flew and the whole island was chaos. They did not bomb the store, but if they had it would not have done us much good. You see, on December 8, there was martial law imposed on the islands and they announced over the radio that anyone caught looting would be shot.

Well that certainly took care of our **free candy.**

FIRST FLIGHT

One thing you must learn is that the history books are not always correct. Many times history credits someone with a great accomplishment when in fact others may have done the deed first.

A good example is the first flight of a heavier than airplane. This was supposed to have been done by the Wright Brothers when in fact it was done by the Wrong Brothers, Weelee, Louie and Joe.

Orville and Wilbur Wright claim this first when they flew an airplane at Kitty Hawk, North Carolina at the turn of the century. They made a plane from wood and a cloth skin to take advantage of weight. They had been bicycle manufacturers so they had good mechanical skills.

Enter the Wrong Brothers!

The Wrong Brothers were three Portagees who came over from the old country to work in the cane fields of Hawaii. They soon got tired of that and decided to find another way to fame.

In the early 1900's there was a lot of interest in flight so Weelee, Louie and Joe decided that they would be the first to fly an airplane. Unlike the Wright Brothers, they decided to build a real strong airplane that would not break up easily.

Louie suggested that they make it from cast iron, since that was really strong. Weelee and Joe agreed, so they built the frame from cast iron. Next came to outer skin. Since a cloth skin would tear easily, Weelee thought that the skin should be made of metal. So they went to a junk yard and got some lead sheet and were able to make the skin and finish the plane. It was a beautiful plane and they were on their way to fame.

Joe found an old engine from a Maytag washing machine and they used that to turn the propeller. Now they were all set.

Since the Wrong Brothers lived in Kaneohe, they figured that the best way to test their airplane was to take it up to the Nuuanu Pali. This is a high cliff with a drop of a thousand feet.

So on the big day, they got their airplane to the edge of the Pali and had a bunch of other Portagees to help push them. They started the engine and all three Wrong Brothers got into the airplane on their way to fame.

The Portagee launchers pushed hard...for some reason this airplane was so heavy. At last it began to roll and headed off the cliff...straight down!

So this was the First Flight of the Wrong Brothers.

Lucky for Weelee, Louie and Joe, a strong gust of wind slowed their plunge and they were thrown from the plane into the guava bushes at the bottom of the Pali, but the plane was a wreck.

So this is the history of the First Flight. The Wrong Brothers finally figured out the problem with their airplane. Louie thought that the engine was too small.

FOOTWASHER

When Grandpa Bigdog was growing up in Hawaii, he lived in Honolulu. This was a big city, which stretched over 50 miles from Diamond Head to near Pearl Harbor.

During the year Uncle Paul and I attended Cathedral School with Eddie Mederios and other friends.

Uncle Joe (Double Rope) had a dairy on the other side of the island near Kailua. This was a large tract of land near the Nuuanu Pali owned by Harold Castle. On this land were a large banana patch, a swamp a small stream and a large milking barn holding 150 milk cows.

Uncle Paul and I used to love to go to the barn and watch the cows. So we would hitch hike from our home on Boyd Lane. We went over to Nuuanu Avenue and waited for rides. One of the dairy owners who had a dairy on the other side of the mountain from Double Rope was a man called Piper. He had a large Fageol truck and if he saw us standing on the road side, would slow down so we could climb on top of his truck which usually had empty milk cans and sacks of feed for his cattle.

When we got to the bottom of the Pali road there was a fork in the road leading to Kaneohe and Kahuku where Miosake lived and to Kailua. Piper slowed his truck, but never stopped so we had to jump off, then hitch another ride to Auntie Annie's house on Hualani Street in Kailua.

Double Rope had a lot of cows. Most of them were large Holsteins, which are black and white cows, which gave a lot of milk. He also had Guernsey, Jersey cows and Ashires. The Jersey cows were the smallest of the cows and they are very beautiful. These cows stand about five feet high and are very tame.

GBD used to have fun with these cows. At milking time these cows were placed in stanchions and we fed them some grain consisting of pineapple bran and oats. As the cows ate, we would milk them.

GBD used to sit on the end of the feed trough and the cow would push me off with her head. GBD would go flying off into space.

At the entrance to the barn there was a large foot washer. This was a concrete trough ten feet wide; fifty feet long and about one foot deep. The cows would walk through this water to wash the mud off their feet as they came into the barn. This water was pretty dirty and smelly and Uncle Paul and GBD used to get invited to clean it and refill it with fresh water.

One day GBD got a great idea. He would get on the back of this Jersey cow and ride her out of the barn. So GBD got on her back and opened the stanchion. The cow backed out and ran for the foot washer with GBD hanging on for dear life. When she got to the foot washer she stopped and GBD went flying over her head right into the dirty water…what a mess.

I'll tell you about other barn stories later.

FRANK'S DOG

When Grandpa Bigdog left the Army, he enrolled in Graduate School at Notre Dame University. Married graduate students could find housing in former prisoner of war barracks that the University purchased for the need. These units consisted of three apartments per unit. We had an apartment on one end, a visiting professor in the middle and an obnoxious Texan on the other end who had a beagle dog.

And that was the problem!

Grandma Bigdog had planted a flower garden and every afternoon when Frank came home from school he would walk right through her flowerbeds. Then he would let his dog out and the dog would run over to our sidewalk and promptly deposit a pile of processed dog food for Michael to walk into.

Well, Grandma Bigdog complained to GBD about this problem, but GBD did not do anything about the problem. But one day, Grandma Bigdog insisted that GBD go over and tell Frank that the dog was messing up our sidewalk and he should stop the practice.

So GBD went over to see Frank. GBD knocked on the door and Frank opened it.

"Frank, your dog is dropping processed dog food on our sidewalk" GBD said.

"That's your problem", Frank said and slammed the door.

When GBD got back to our apartment, Grandma Bigdog wanted to know what he said and GBD told her.

"What are we going to do then?" Grandma Bigdog asked.

"Nothing, until tomorrow at one o'clock" said GBD.

So GBD went back to the chemistry laboratory and synthesized a large batch of nitrogen triiodide, a very loud explosive that is so shock sensitive that if a fly landed on it, it would explode with a loud **BANG** with a purple cloud rising up in the air.

The next day GBD came home at noon and waited. Then GBD spread the explosive across the sidewalk and sat in the house to see what would develop. Sure enough just about one o'clock here comes obnoxio walking through the flowerbed and to his apartment. He let his dog out and the dog sped for our sidewalk.

BANG! BANG! BANG!...YIPE, YIPE, YIPE! as the poor dog ran for home. Frank came flying out of the apartment, but we stayed put.

For some reason, the dog never came over to our sidewalk again.

GAMES

What kind of games do you play? I know you have cars, Nintendo games and lots of robots and toys that you have gotten as gifts or bought with your own money.

But what if you did not have any money to buy toys? What would you do? Well, Grandpa Bigdog did not have any money when he was a little boy and neither did Uncle Paul or the kids we played with. So we played games that required little money such as marbles, cops and robbers, hide and seek or anything we could think up.

Marble games were a lot of fun and we played many of these. Did you play marble games? Here are some of the games GBD played: BOX, RING, and FISH.

For BOX we would make a rectangular box with a stick in the dirt about 3 feet by 5 feet and near one end draw a small line 6 inches long and put two marbles on each end of the line. Then we would shoot with our KEENE (the marble we used to shoot with we called the KEENE. If we would hit one of the marbles off the line, we then could chase the other guys KEENE and if we hit it, he would have to give me a marble. In this way GBD or Uncle Paul could acquire more marbles.

In RING we would make a circle about 3 feet in diameter and in the middle of the circle we would place some marbles. For example, GBD would put in 10 marbles and Uncle Paul 10 marbles. Then from the edge of the circle (ring) we would shoot our KEENE and try to knock marbles out of the ring with out the KEENE getting stuck outside the ring. The marbles we knocked out we would keep. If our KEENE rolled out of the ring we would lose our turn.

Another game was FISH that was similar to ring. Here we drew a fish in the dirt and from a line back away from the fish we would shoot our KEENE to see if we could knock marbles out of the FISH without the KEENE getting stuck in the fish. If the KEENE got stuck in the fish, we would lose our turn.

GBD and Uncle Paul used to spend hours playing these games with our friends, Pig, Guava, Abage, Walter and Eddie Mederios. What we tried to avoid was letting girls play because they were always better and would end up winning all our marbles.

Another game we played was CAPS. In those days (1934) milk was delivered in glass bottles and capped with a round paper cap. We used to collect these especially since they had different designs on them. What we would do is pile 5 caps from GBD and 5 from Uncle Paul and hit the pile with a KEENE that in this case was a milk cap. If the pile turned over, we would keep the caps that fell off the pile and that way we could add to our collection of caps.

Uncle Joe (Double Rope) had a dairy and once in a while he would give Uncle Paul and GBD a stack of new caps and we were the envy of our friends. Since they were new they would let us hit harder and turn more caps over and we would win more games.

So much for these games. GBD will have to tell you about the broomstick games and the time Uncle Paul and GBD had a big sling shot fight with Uncle Wally. But we can hold that for another time. [See Sling Shot]

Don't forget your KEENE and we can play marbles sometime.

GRAVE YARD TALES: THE FUNERAL

This is a story about a very grave matter. When Grandpa was a little boy, we lived on Awaiolimu Street in Honolulu. At the end of the road was a dead end on the edge of Papakulea where a Hawaiian village was located. Also located there were four, yes four graveyards. The Chinese grave yard was on the right facing the slopes of Punchbowl…a volcanic crater. Dead ahead was a Korean grave yard, to the left a Japanese grave yard and over Pauoa stream a Hawaiian grave yard.

One of the most terrifying experiences that Uncle Paul and I had was when there was a Chinese Funeral. The Funeral procession would wind up Awaiolimu Street with flute players making strange sounds. Behind the hearse which carried the departed person, were the mourners who wore burlap hoods and scared the daylights out of all the little kids. But worse of all was the hearse. The driver of the hearse and his attendant held out their hands that contained small sheets of tissue paper having holes punched into the sheets. They would let these sheets fall and the wind scattered them along the path of the funeral procession. If one of these sheets landed on one of us we would let out a big scream and run away. The idea of these papers and the holes was that the evil spirits had to find all of these sheets and pass through the holes to get to the soul of the departed. So whenever we heard the flutes and saw a funeral procession coming up the street, we would run and hide.

GRAVE YARD TALES: THE OPEN GRAVE

This is a story about a very grave matter. When Grandpa Bigdog was a little boy, we lived on Awaiolimu Street in Honolulu. At the end of the road was a dead end on the edge of Papakulea where a Hawaiian village was located. Also located there were four, yes four graveyards. The Chinese graveyard was on the right facing the slopes of Punchbowl...a volcanic crater. Dead ahead was a Korean graveyard, to the left a Japanese graveyard and over Pauoa stream a Hawaiian graveyard.

One night after supper just before the sun went down, Uncle Paul and I and our pal who we called Pig and a few other boys decided to walk up to the top of Punchbowl. One of the kids was rich, that is, he had more money than Uncle Paul and I had so that he could afford to go to see a movie. So to get to the top of Punchbowl, we walked up Awaiolimu Street to the Chinese grave yard. There we walked past the tombstones and up to a wall where we climbed up to Puowaina Drive. From there we continued up to the top of Punchbowl crater.

Soon the sunset! In Hawaii, when the sun sets, it gets real dark immediately...no twilight like you have in Iowa. So we sat on a high point in the crater and the boy who went to the movie began to tell us about the picture. It was Frankenstein and the Werewolf. He talked about how the man turned into a Werewolf when the full moon came out. We were all terrified as he related to details of this horror movie. As we were now completely scared, the full moon rose out of the ocean by Diamond Head. Soon dark clouds covered the moon and we all decided we had enough. So we started back down the mountain. Since it was so dark we were all bumping into each other afraid to be the last in line where we might get caught by the Werewolf.

As we neared the top of the Chinese graveyard, Uncle Paul and I kept asking the older kids to walk home with us. They said sure, but when we got to the top of the stonewall, all we heard was "Goodnight" and they left us standing there in the dark. Uncle Paul and I were now terrified, because we had to walk through the Chinese graveyard to get home. So we finally decided to climb down the stonewall and run for our lives through the graveyard. As we were tripping over tombstones, Grandpa fell into an open grave.

To this day I don't know how I ever got out of that grave. I must have just leaped straight out, because when we got home Great Grandma Olivia saw two small boys, white as sheets pounding on the front door.

GRAVE YARD TALES: FALLING ASLEEP

This is another story about a very grave matter. When Grandpa was a little boy, we lived on Awaiolimu Street in Honolulu. At the end of the road was a dead end on the edge of Papakulea where a Hawaiian village was located. Also located there were four, yes four graveyards. The Chinese graveyard was on the right facing the slopes of Punchbowl...a volcanic crater. Dead ahead was a Korean graveyard, to the left a Japanese graveyard and over Pauoa stream a Hawaiian graveyard.

Uncle Wally used to raise rabbits. So every day he would go out with a gunny sack and pick weeds called puleileis to feed his bunnies. The best place to pick puleileis was in the Grave Yard at the end of Awaiolimu street. So after school he would take a gunny sack or two and head out for the grave yard to pick weeds. He usually got one or two sacks full and carried them home.

One day, uncle Wally went out to pull weeds. On this day there were not too many puleileis in the Chinese grave yard, so he went over by Pauoa stream and the Hawaiian grave yard. There he found a lot of weeds and began to fill his sack. It was getting late in the afternoon and Uncle Wally got sleepy, so he set his sack down and fell asleep.

Unfortunately, it soon got dark and he woke up and looked around only to find tombstones all around him. He jumped up and ran as fast as he could to get home. He even forgot his puleileis, but never went back to get them until the next day.

So sleeping on the job was not a good idea.

GRAVE YARD TALES: CRIME DOESN'T PAY

This is a story about a very grave matter. When Grandpa was a little boy, we lived on Awaiolimu Street in Honolulu. At the end of the road was a dead end on the edge of Papakulea where a Hawaiian village was located. Also located there were four, yes four graveyards. The Chinese graveyard was on the right facing the slopes of Punchbowl...a volcanic crater. Dead ahead was a Korean graveyard, to the left a Japanese graveyard and over Pauoa stream a Hawaiian graveyard.

When there was a Chinese funeral Uncle Paul, our friend Pig and other kids used to go to the grave yard and watch the ceremony. After the ceremony, the people in the funeral party would stand at the gates of the graveyard and hand out little pieces of red paper containing nickels, dimes or quarters. So we would get behind a mourner and put our hands out and get a coin. Then we would climb over the stonewall and go back through the line again. In this way we could get some money.

On this day, I was able to get 35 cents in coins and Uncle Paul got 85 cents. We then went home and had lunch. During lunch Uncle Paul and I began shaking the coins in our pockets to brag to Great Grandma Olivia that we had money. She then asked us where we got this money and we told her. Great Grandma Olivia got angry at us for stealing money from the dead and she made us go to church and put the money in the poor box. You must realize that this was big money. For example, we could buy a loaf of bread for 10 cents or go to a movie for 10 cents and to give up this fortune was a real punishment for our crime.

So Uncle Paul and I then walked down to the Blessed Sacrament Church on Pauoa Avenue to put the money in the poor box.

So you see that when you do something wrong, you can't really get away with it.

GOODNIGHT!!

When Grandpa Bigdog lived in Honolulu, our family attended Our Lady of Peace Church on Fort Street. Later on the church built a new church on Pauoa Street nearer our home on Boyd Lane. This church was named Blessed Sacrament Church.

Grandpa Bigdog was an altar boy at this church and Fr. Gregory Rotier was our priest. A number of my friends were also altar boys. There were Peter Gomez and his brother, and Joe Keenee a Hawaiian boy who lived on the slopes of Punchbowl in a very small house, just up the street from Boogo on Puowaina Drive. GBD can remember that Joe's father used to plant sweet potatoes in their garden.

Well, one day poor Joe's parents died and Joe had to go live with his uncle on Nuuanu Avenue.

One of the many tasks altar boys had to do at Blessed Sacrament Church was to serve at 7:30 mass in the morning and to serve at Sunday masses. This was done by rotation so that everyone got a chance to serve. We also served at Holy Hour and during lent on Friday night for the Stations of the Cross. This was usually at 7 in the evening and lasted about an hour.

Now, back to Joe Keenee. GBD mentioned that Joe went to live with his uncle. His uncle was the caretaker of the cemetery on Nuuanu Avenue near the hill where Eddie Medeiros had the accident with the sewer covers. This cemetery was a large place and Joe's uncle lived at the far back of the cemetery.

One night GBD was serving at the Stations of the Cross with Joe Keenee and Peter Gomez and some other boys. After the service Joe asked GBD if he wanted to go out and play before curfew. (There was a nine o'clock curfew in Honolulu and we all had to be off the streets when the siren sounded at the Aloha Tower).

So GBD agreed to go with Joe, but he told GBD that he had to stop by his house to get something before we could go out to play. Well we walked over to Nuuanu Avenue then up to the entrance to the cemetery and it was now pitch dark. In order to get to Joe's uncle's home we had to walk diagonally through the cemetery to the very end. It was real scary and Joe kept mentioning how scared he was. When we finally reached the end of the cemetery, there was a large hibiscus hedge surrounding the house. Joe disappeared into the hedge and said, "Goodnight".

What Joe had done was to trick me into walking home with him, because he was afraid of walking through the cemetery alone.

Now what?

GBD was really scared and began walking back toward Nuuanu Avenue and tripping over gravestones. Finally, GBD walked across the cemetery to a side street, climbed the stonewall there and made it to a dark street. From there GBD ran as fast as he could till he reached Nuuanu Avenue and safety.

That was sure a dirty trick to play on another altar boy and one GBD will never forget!

UNCLE WALLY'S ARK

In biblical times, God decided to flood the earth to punish the evil people who lived on earth. There was a just man named Noah and his family who God decided to save from drowning. So God told Noah to build an ark, which was a large boat so that Noah and a lot of animals and birds could be saved.

In Hawaii we have a lot of rain. Most of the homes there are built with tin roofs that are made from sheets of corrugated steel. The steel sheets are nailed to the roof with big roofing nails. During a rain shower, you can hear the rain hitting the tin roof and making a lot of noise. Sometimes the wind blows a sheet of tin roof off and it has to be replaced.

Behind our house on Awaiolimu street is Pauoa stream, a small river where we used to fish and swim. We also built a dam on the stream from stones that made a big pond behind the dam.

One day Uncle Wally decided to make a boat. So he found a piece of tin roof and bent it into a shape of a boat. At the front of boat he nailed a two by four piece of wood to make the bow and at the back a piece of wood that would hold nails to form the back or stern of the boat. Since this was an old piece of tin roof there were nail holes that had to be patched to keep water out of the boat. So, how do we patch the nail holes?

Well, it gets pretty hot in Honolulu and in the afternoon the heat of the sun melts tar on the road, so Uncle Wally scraped up some tar and patched the nail holes on his ark. Then came the big event...launch the boat in Pauoa stream. With a lot of kids around, Uncle Wally pushed his boat into the pond and got in. The boat nearly capsized, but he was able to keep it level. Then amid the cheers of his fans, he paddled out into the pond.

Unfortunately for Uncle Wally, he patched the nail holes from the inside of the boat and soon the pressure of the water popped the tar loose and the boat began to fill with water and sank.

So, unlike Noah and his ark, Uncle Wally was not so lucky.

GRANDPA AND GRAMMA BIGDOG

HAM SANDWICH

When Grandpa Bigdog was growing up in Campbell, California, he lived on 16 Foote Street in a house that belonged to GBD' s grandfather Manuel Miranda. He was a great man and one of the best wine makers in Santa Clara Valley.

GBD worked his way through college as a movie projectionist in the Campbell Theater. This was a converted bank building and GBD spent many hours running movies. One of the good advantages of that job was that it allowed GBD the opportunity to study while working.

GBD did this for many years and finally graduated in 1951 from San Jose State College. After graduation, GBD went on to Graduate School and worked on a Master's degree.

(Becky, Matthew, Susan and Nicky do you know anyone else in our family who have Master's Degrees?)

35

After graduating again in 1952, GBD was offered a teaching position at San Jose State College teaching Chemistry, Physics, Astronomy and Geology.

Well, all of a sudden GBD went from being a student to being a teacher and had to get started in his new career.

GBD lived at home with Great Grandma Olivia and Aunt Lorraine, who was also a student at San Jose State College.

So the first day of school in September 1952, GBD dressed up like a used car salesman and headed off to his first class, Chemistry 1A.

There were quite a few students in the class and GBD announced that if the students needed help, they could come to the office.

One of GBD's students was Carol Mott. She came to the office to learn about the slide rule and to work on chemistry problems, but she was the best student in the class.

GG Olivia used to fix GBD peanut butter sandwiches, so after class GBD would go to the office and eat lunch. One day GG Olivia told GBD that she would make him a ham sandwich for a change.

All during class GBD could only think of the ham sandwich. As soon as class was over, GBD went to his office. As usual, here came Carol Mott with her usual questions.

GBD answered her questions and wondered how soon she would leave so he could devour his ham sandwich.

Well, she lingered on and on. Finally, GBD asked if she would like a piece of my sandwich, thinking that she would eat half and leave half for GBD.

Well, you guessed it...she ate the whole thing as GBD sat there stunned.

So be careful when you share your lunch. In GBD's case, he wound up marrying his student...the greatest thing GBD ever did.

HOLY GHOST HILL

When Grandpa was a young boy, he lived in Honolulu near Punchbowl, an extinct volcano. As a result there were many steep streets along the slopes of Punchbowl.

Grandpa lived near Lusitana Street on a small lane called Boyd Lane. Near Boyd Lane was another lane named Bush Lane. Across the street from Bush Lane was Grandpa's great friend Eddie Medeiros. And just two houses down from Eddie's house was Holy Ghost Hill.

Holy Ghost Hill is actually Concordia street and at the top of the street is a Holy Ghost Chapel. Holy Ghost Hill was so steep, that it was difficult to ride a bike up the hill. To ride a bike to the top, Eddie and I used to ride back and forth across the street to make it to the top. But, once at the top it was a great ride down and the bikes would just fly down the hill.

Enter Blanche Teves. She was a pretty girl and cousin of Freddie Baboose and Howard Santos. Grandpa liked her and was interested in trying to impress her at every opportunity. Well, one day that opportunity came, but it was not the opportunity Grandpa thought it would be.

It so happened that there was a bus stop at the bottom of Holy Ghost Hill and Blanche was waiting for the bus. Grandpa was riding Uncle Wally's famous bike and decided to show off to Blanche. So he pushed the bike to the top of Holy Ghost Hill and thought that he could ride the bike down the hill.

Only to make a big impression, Grandpa decided to ride down Holy Ghost Hill by standing on the seat and once he got to Lusitana Street he would swing down Bush Lane.

So Grandpa rode past Blanche a couple of times then pushed the bike up to the top of Holy Ghost Hill. Then like a big circus hero (dunce) Grandpa stood up on the seat and roared down the hill. When he got to the bottom of the hill, he waved to Blanche and steered the bike down Bush Lane. What Grandpa did not know was that they had just spread gravel all over the lane and there were speed bumps in the lane. After hitting the first bump Grandpa lost control of the bike and went skidding all over the gravel. The noise was so loud Uncle Paul could hear the accident over on Boyd Lane.

Well, Grandpa picked up the bike and pushed it up to the top of the lane, only to find that the bus had come and Blanche was nowhere to be found. So showing off got Grandpa a lot of scrapes and a banged up bike.

UNCLE PAUL AT HOLY GHOST CHAPEL

IMPRESS THE GIRLS

When Grandpa was growing up in Hawaii, he spent a lot of time riding a bike all over Honolulu.   Grandpa's good friend Eddie Mederios was always riding with me.

Eddie and I really enjoyed riding our bikes and as soon as school was out, he and I would grab our bikes and ride. There were a lot of good places to ride.

There was of course Holy Ghost Hill that was a real challenge since it was so steep. Another good street was Puowaina Drive. This street ran all the way up to the top of Punchbowl and the ride down was really fast and easy, since it was all down hill.

Some of the stunts we used to pull were to ride off a curb or jump curve stones. We used to also ride down the steps of the Buddhist Temple on Emma Street.

Eddie was a daredevil and an ordained show off. One day we were riding bike near an abandoned Japanese churchyard. In the yard was an abandoned fishpond with a concrete frame around the pond that was about a foot wide. The water level was down about five feet from the top of the pond and contained some very foul smelling water.

So Eddie decided to try riding his bike on the ledge of the pool, with the gang urging him on. Well Eddie set the bike up on the ledge and began his tight rope ride. He made it past the first turn to the cheers of the crowd, including Grandpa, Uncle Paul and Eddie's brothers Walter and Johnnie. Then Eddie made it around the second turn to more cheers...but on the third turn the back wheel slipped and down went Eddie and his bike into the foul smelling water. So we all reached over the wall to help Eddie out of that sewer.

Another time Grandpa and Eddie were riding our bikes up Kanealii street. This was a long sloping street with many cross streets along the way. As we got up to Naone street there were some girls sitting along the corner on the grass. So Eddie decided that we should put on a show for them. He suggested we ride to the top of Kanealii street and ride down standing on the seat. His plan was that when we got to Naone street we would turn our bikes onto Naone street and wave at the girls.

So far so good...

So we peddled all the up to the end of the street. The way the road was built it was shaped like a stairway. Every crossroad caused the bikes to go faster so it was like getting a shove each time we went over a crossroad.

So down came the two clowns for the big show off. We were going to impress the girls. We peddled as hard as we could then stood up on the bikes with our arms outstretched and steered the bikes down the hill.

For some reason Grandpa was a bit ahead of Eddie and I got near the girls and I leaned over and steered the bike onto Naone street and waved at the girls.

Here comes Eddie. He too was waving at the girls but he made a wider curve than I did and the front wheel of his bike hit the curb and sent Eddie flying in the air and he landed on the grass.

He really impressed the girls...they were laughing so hard that they missed seeing him pick up his bike as Grandpa Bigdog and Eddie made a beeline for Pauoa street and home.

So much for impressing the girls.

THE SLED

When Grandpa Bigdog was a boy, he lived in Hawaii along with his brothers Paul and Wally. In school he would read about snow and how boys and girls would ride sleds in the snow. But, in Hawaii, there is no snow (except on a very high mountains on the Island of Hawaii...called Mauna Kea and Mauna Loa). Mauna Kea means White Mountain and Mauna Loa means Long Mountain and it is the largest volcano in the world.

Uncle Paul and GBD lived on the slopes of a volcanic crater and the sides of the volcano are very steep. GBD and Uncle Paul used to spend a lot of time climbing the slopes of this volcano, which was called Punchbowl because it was shaped like a large punch bowl.

The slopes of the volcano were covered with a waxy grass. One day GBD got an idea. He wondered if he could make a sled like they used for snow sledding. GBD was a lousy carpenter, but Uncle Paul was good at woodwork, so he built a sled out of wood and cut runners on the bottom.

Punchbowl was also covered with cactus plants and we found out that if they cut open a cactus leaf…very carefully because there are large thorns on the cactus…they could get a wax out of the cactus to put on the runners of the sled.

GBD and Uncle Paul then took the sled to Punchbowl and began riding the sled down the slopes. The sled went so fast, that we had to roll off the sled when we got to the bottom of the slope. Soon our friends began to build sleds and were riding down the mountain.

People began to come to see "sled riding in the tropics". One day GBD, Uncle Paul and their friend Pig (that was his nickname) were riding down the slopes when a newspaper photographer took our picture. The next day, our picture was in the Honolulu Star Bulletin…on the FRONT PAGE.

So you see what a little idea can become if you follow through and do something about it.

KANAKAS EVERYWHERE

When Grandpa was a young boy he lived on the slopes of Punchbowl, an extinct crater in Honolulu. Grandpa and Uncle Paul found a way to make bobsleds from wood and slide down the steep slopes of the volcano. Since the volcano was covered with grass we had to smash the grass down to make a trail down the mountain. Once we established a trail, it was smooth sailing and we really flew down the mountain. This was great except…

There were some hazards in the way of our fun. You see there were guava stumps in the grass and if we hit them we would go flying off the sled. This was not bad except that there were pinene bushes all over the slopes. Pinene bushes are cactus plants full of sharp thorns and if you landed in one of them it would really see stars. Another hazard were the Kanakas.

Above Punchbowl on the slopes of Mt. Tantalus was a Hawaiian settlement. We called them Kanakas, which is a Hawaiian name for Hawaiian men. The Kanakas also were not too friendly to Uncle Paul and Grandpa. Every time we would spend hours making a trail, they would come along and drive us off and take over our trail. One day just after we made a new trail they came along, twelve of them and drove us off. So, Uncle Paul came up with a great idea.

A few days later, Uncle Paul and I took our sled up the mountain and began the slow process of making a new slide trail. It was steep and we really had a good time, but at the end of the trail was a large guava stump hidden in the grass and a huge clump of pinenes at the end of the trail. So Uncle Paul figured that we could slide down and just before we got to the stump, we would roll off the sled into the grass, because if we hit the stump, we would fly into the pinenes and see a lot of stars. This worked so well we had a great time until...**the Kanakas showed up.**

About ten of them with a large sled made from two by fours came up dragging the huge sled behind them. They told us to scram or else. Uncle Paul in turn told them that he would give them a push to get started. So the sled loaded with ten kanakas went roaring down the trail all laughing until they hit the guava stump and went flying into the pinenes!

Meanwhile, Uncle Paul and Grandpa ran for our lives to the sound of screams from the cactus thorns as the Kanakas got their just desserts.

GRANDPA BIGDOG AND AUNTIE LORRAINE

LORRAINE GO HOME...

When Grandpa Bigdog was growing up in Hawaii he and the family lived on welfare. Great Grandma Bigdog had only $50.00 a month to feed all five children. As a result, we had little money to buy toys like the children of today.

So, Uncle Paul and GBD had to rely on our wits to make toys with which to play. We made slingshots, stick toys from broom handles, kites from bamboo trees and skate cars.

Now the skate car was our regal toy. Since we had no skates or could not buy any, we scrounged around in junk piles looking for something to use for play. One day, Uncle Paul found a single skate.

This was a real find and we were on our way to real fun!

Uncle Paul took the skate apart and recovered four wheels. He then began to make a skate car. He took a piece of wood and nailed a 2x2 on the back, then a piece of 1x4 to the bottom. Then on the front of the skate car he attached a 2x2 with a hole in the center to make the skate car steerable. Now, Uncle Paul needed axles for the wheels. To accomplish this he used four spikes, which we found where they were building a house on Whiting Street.

Uncle Paul slid the spike into the wheel, then bent the end of the spike and fastened it to the 2x2 using fence nails which we got from Uncle Joe's (Double Rope) dairy.

We were now ready to test the car, so GBD, Uncle Paul and Aunt Lorraine headed for Kuakini Street for the test run. As usual, Uncle Paul went first and roared down Kuakini Street until he hit a bump in the sidewalk and fell off the skate car.

What we needed was a better surface, so we decided to find a long steep hill. We went up Holy Ghost Hill to Puowaina Drive, which was a long sloping road that wrapped around Punchbowl and ran down to Lusitana Street.

Uncle Paul and GBD got on the skate car and had a nice long ride down the street until we hit a bump and the wheel came off. What had happened was the fence nails had slipped out and the wheel came off.

"Lorraine Go Home and get us some nails for the axle", Uncle Paul said. So Lorraine walked up Lusitana Street past Mrs. Freitas and Eddie Medeiros houses to our home on Boyd Lane. There she picked up a hammer and some fence nails and came back.

Soon Uncle Paul had the skate car fixed and we sailed down Puowaina Drive till it joined Lusitana Street near Kunimoto's store where we bought our groceries.

GBD and Uncle Paul were so lucky to have Aunt Lorraine help us fix our skate car.

You cannot imagine how much fun we had with skate cars and how we appreciated having our mechanic (Aunt Lorraine) standing by.

SS HUALALAI
Thomas J. Miranda

When Grandpa Bigdog lived in Honolulu, there were few means of rapid transportation. There was an inter island airplane which flew to Hilo and Maui and the major means for inter island transportation was by ship. There were two ships that plied the waters around Oahu, the SS Hualalai and the SS Waialiali.

The Hualalai traveled from Honolulu to Lahiana, Maui then onto Hilo. The Waialiali traveled to Kauai and we could always note the departure, since the ship blew its whistle around 9:00 pm at night and headed off to Kauai. The Hualalai left around 5:00 pm, stopped in Lahaina and arrived in Hilo in the early morning. These ships were about 325 feet long and were the mainstay of inter island transportation by sea.

When GBD was six years old, Auntie Maria came to Honolulu on a visit and she offered to take me back with her. So one afternoon we went down to near the Aloha Tower where the SS Hualalai was moored. We did not exactly go first class, but rode steerage that is in the very stern of the ship. The ship left about 5 in the afternoon and headed out past Diamond Head on toward Maui. There were a lot of ropes curled on the deck and you could hear the loud noise of the engine as we plowed on into the sunset. Some where around nine o'clock the ship reached Lahaina, Maui where passengers and cargo were unloaded and other passengers embarked and then we were off to Hawaii.

The next morning we approached the big island as the ship moved closer to Hilo, the main city in Hawaii. When the ship docked we went to Auntie Maria and Uncle John's house in Hilo. I remember staying there a few days and visited Uncle John and Auntie Bella, then we were off to Kukaiau Ranch were Uncle Manuel and Auntie Ida lived with their children Abel, Daniel, Bella and Lydia.

Kukaiau Ranch is on the slopes of Mauna Kea, a large volcano and the highest mountain in Hawaii and the ranch is high in the clouds near the top of the mountain. GBD remembers cousin Able showing me his pet pig that he let out of the pen and chased around the yard. Uncle Manuel was a master craftsman and most likely the best saddle maker on the island. Since they had a lot of cattle and horses on the ranch it was important that there were good saddles and bridles and Uncle Manuel's were the best.

One day cousin Abel and GBD rode a horse up the mountainside through some eucalyptus forest when we came upon a wild turkey with a brood of chicks. We got off the horse and chased the chicks until we rounded up 18 chicks. We thought we really had a great find until the mother turkey came flying at us, we dropped the chicks and ran for the horse and rode away.

There were many horses on the ranch and GBD had a great time riding horses. One day GBD got on a horse and rode up to the stable. Cousin Daniel, Uncle Manuel's son, decided to play a trick on GBD and turned the saddle backwards on the horse. Needless to say that was hard to ride. After I put up a fuss he returned the saddle to the correct way, then I rode the horse back down the road past Uncle Adolph's house. When GBD turned the horse around the horse took off and ran toward the stable. GBD got scared and threw the bridle away and hung on to the pommel (saddle horn). Auntie Ida was watching out the window of her house and wondered why I was riding so fast, but I couldn't stop the horse. When we reached the gate, the horse suddenly stopped and GBD got down. That was enough horseback riding for one day.

Auntie Ida had a Maytag washing machine on the lower level of the house powered by a gasoline engine. GBD had never seen one before and thought that was unusual. GBD remembers that the exhaust pipe ran under ground and came out near the road.

Another thing that was unusual was the fog. Since Kukaiau Ranch is so high, clouds form around Mauna Kea and this creates a dense fog that sweeps down the mountain and is really strange. It was difficult to see and sometimes the cloud lingered for a long time.

After leaving the ranch, GBD spent some time with Auntie Nora in Honokaa. Uncle Alfred ran a grocery store and we were always so grateful to them because each year at Christmas, Uncle Alfred sent a big box with candy and goodies for us.

One day GBD and cousin Ella had a penny each and Auntie Nora told us not to spend it on candy. Well Ella and I went to the store and bought licorice suckers and began eating them in the back yard. When Auntie Nora called us, we hid the candy under some wood and went into the house. She asked us if we had bought candy and we lied, "No". But since the licorice was black, our faces were all smeared with black candy and that gave us away.

One day Uncle Ernest Awong took us down to see Auntie Mary at Haina. There is a big sugar mill and we got to see how they crushed cane to make sugar. There were huge crushing wheels that crushed the cane stalks. We also went by the rail cars and pulled cane stalks from the cars and cut off pieces of cane to chew. That is really delicious.

Finally, GBD went back on the SS Hualalai to Honolulu. That was a trip I shall never forget.

Uncle Manuel and Auntie Ida's home on Kukaiau Ranch

THE MILKSTOOL

When Grandpa Bigdog was growing up in Hawaii, he used to love to go to Auntie Annie's place in Kailua. She lived in the coconut grove and had a big yard. Uncle Joe [Double Rope] had a few cows there which cousin Peter or Walter would milk each day. Cousin Peter had a large black cow he named Babe.

Uncle Paul and I used to take her down to Kaulani Way where there were a lot of guava bushes and a lot of grass so she could graze all daylong. We also had to be careful with Babe because she would hook us with her horns is we got too close to her.

Cousin Peter was the only one who could milk her without being kicked.

Double Rope had a large dairy near the Pali and we used to go there to watch them milk the cows and we helped clean the barn and put grain in the troughs when the cows were being milked.

In those days Double Rope milked his cows by hand and there were a few tricks needed to successfully milk a cow, also some hazards. For example, the cow had to be milked from the right side. Some of the cows would kick when we tried to milk them, so we would have to tie a rope

45

around their back legs to prevent them from kicking. After milking we had to grab our milk stool with one hand and the milk bucket with the other and get away from the cow as soon as possible.

One cow had a peculiar habit of waiting till she was fully milked then would put her right leg into the milk bucket when GBD was trying to get up. This did not make Double Rope too happy.

Some of the meaner cows needed leg chains to constrain them while milking. This was a steel cuff fitted over the cows back legs.

Another hazard was the cow's tail When the cow was trying to shoo flies, she would swish her tail around and usually hit us on the face or head and that would sting.

Each of us had a milking stool. We usually made these from wooden boxes that we found. Some of these were stronger and were made with 2x8 wood and a firm top.

Well, one day GBD decided to make a new milk stool. After working a long time on it he finally had a brand new milk stool and couldn't wait to get to the barn to try it out.

Double Rope knew which cows were dangerous to milk so he let GBD milk only certain cows who were not prone to kicking. One Holstein cow was a marginal kicker and a loose rope would be enough to keep her from kicking.

Since GBD had a new milk stool he wasn't taking chances and used a chain on the poor cows legs. Well everything was fine until she began to bawl and started kicking her back legs. GBD grabbed the milk bucket and ran just as she came down right on the new milk stool and crushed it. Double Rope took off the chain and scolded GBD for doing that.

I picked up my flattened milk stool and walked away.

UNCLE WALLY

46

MIOSAKE

When Grandpa Bigdog was growing up in Hawaii he lived in Honolulu on the slopes of Punchbowl, an extinct volcano. Honolulu was a big city and we were thus city dwellers.

Enter Uncle Joe. Uncle Paul and I called Uncle Joe "Double Rope". He earned this title because he always told us boys that if we did not behave, he would take a double rope and whack us on the legs.

Uncle Joe was a real tough guy and strong as a horse. He owned a dairy on the other side of the Pali. (The Pali is a high mountain peak that divides the island of Oahu in two). On the other side of the Pali, Uncle Joe had his dairy where he milked about 130 cows twice a day.

Uncle Paul and I used to love to go to the dairy and watch the cows. Eventually, GBD learned how to milk cows and got so good that one day I milked 36 cows, all by hand.

Uncle Joe had a mixture of cows. There were Holstein cows that are large black and white cows that give lots of milk. He also had Guernsey cows that were red and white and Jersey cows which were fawn colored and small cows, about five feet high.

Uncle Joe's barn was near a swamp and we had to be sure that the cows did not go into the swamp and drink the water because of liver flukes in the swamp water.

Enter Miosake!!

Uncle Joe did business with a Japanese man named Miosake. He lived near Kahuku and his cows were also near a swamp. He would come over and try to sell cows to Uncle Joe and Uncle Joe would usually buy a cow from him. Unfortunately, after a few weeks the poor cow died from liver flukes and Miosake couldn't figure why the cow died.

One day Uncle Paul and GBD were playing near the barn when we saw a big Packard car coming down the dirt road leading to Uncle Joe's barn.

We quickly ran to the barn and told Uncle Joe that Miosake had driven into the barnyard. When we went back out, there was Miosake in his

Packard car with a Jersey bull in the back seat. He proceeded to pull the bull out of the car and walk him over to "Double Rope".

"Look Joe", Miosake said, "I got a nice bull to sell you.

Uncle Joe laughed at Miosake. "Look at my big cows and you bring me a small Jersey bull?" No sale.

So Miosake opened the door of his Packard and started loading the bull into the back seat. Uncle Paul and I were on one end pulling the rope and Miosake was behind the bull pushing him back into the car.

Can you just imagine what that looked like...the poor bull was so confused and Miosake lost a sale.

MRS. PAGE'S GARDEN

When Grandpa Bigdog was in high school, he had a 1927 Model T Ford he bought from Mervin Nelson for $5.00. This car did not run too often and GBD used to spent lots of time trying to fix it.

This car did not have a muffler and it could be heard all over Campbell. When GBD could get it started he would drive it to school.

One of GBD's friends was Nina Page. GBD really liked her a lot and was always trying to impress her, but she couldn't care less.

One night GBD went over to the Congregational Church on Central Avenue to pick up Mac Martin and CD Cutting. They had gone to an evening service and it ended about 8:00pm. So we began riding around town in the Model T when GBD got a great idea!!!

"Let's go by Nina Page's house" he suggested. Mac and CD agreed and off we went up Hamilton Avenue and turned onto Winchester Avenue making a lot of noise. Nina had a circular driveway in her yard so GBD turned in and struck the curb so hard that it broke the headlights on the car. The next thing we knew we were driving all over Mrs. Page's flower garden.

The next day we had Chemistry lab and GBD was anxious to tell Nina that I had come by last night...when I overheard her tell Bonnie Decker that some lunatic drove all over her mother's flower bed last night.

Grandpa Bigdog was very quiet and hoped that she would never find out what I had done.

OLE'S CAR

Uncle Wally had an old Model T sedan and he used to drive around Kailua with this car. Some of the kids used to like to jump onto the running board and hang onto the car. So to prevent this Uncle Wally wired a Ford ignition coil to the car. The Ford coil could generate 25,000 volts of electricity and give you quite a jolt. Uncle Wally had a switch on the dashboard to activate the coil so if someone would lean on the car he could turn on the switch and give them a surprise.

When Grandpa Bigdog was going to college, he worked as a movie projectionist at the Sunnyvale Theater in California. The doorman who took tickets bought a new Plymouth car and was very proud of his car. He parked it across the street from the theater where he could watch it. Across the street was a pool hall and the Nobel Laureates who frequented the pool hall would lean up against his car, making Ole very unhappy. He mentioned this to Grandpa Bigdog who suggested a fix for his problem.

GBD remembered what Uncle Wally had done to his model T and he had a Ford coil. So he told Ole that if he came by tomorrow GBD would wire his car with a Ford coil and put a switch on the dash. [The only problem was that GBD did not know how to wire the coil as Uncle Wally did.]

So next day Ole and a friend show up at GBD's house and he put a switch on the dash board and taped the Ford coil to the steering column. To get the biggest spark, GBD had to adjust the coil and you could hear…**dee, dee, dee** as the coil vibrated. So GBD told Ole to turn on the switch so he could adjust the coil.

So GBD began adjusting the coil,…**dee,dee,dee**…**dee,dee,dee** and the car began to shake violently as Grandpa Bigdog tried to adjust the coil. Finally GBD looked up and there was Ole and Jackie bouncing all over the car trying to turn off the switch. Finally GBD disconnected the coil and the two victims jumped out of the car, white as sheets.

You see GBD had reversed the wires and gave them the shock instead.

PICKLES

When Grandpa Bigdog moved from Honolulu to Campbell, California in September of 1942, the first thing he did was to obtain a position as a retail executive at the Sprouse-Reitz 5 and 10 cents store. This important position involved sweeping the floor and taking care of the stock room at the back of the store. This position paid 25 cents per hour.

On my first day on the job, the manager went to lunch and left 65 cents in loose change on top of his desk to test my honesty. When he returned from lunch the money was still there and I noticed a different attitude toward me. I held this executive position for a year until one day the manager told me that they couldn't afford my high salary and was going to promote me out (English for firing me). In my exit interview he told me that the Red and White Store across the street could use me, so I went there and assumed another executive position, now in the food business and a whopping salary of 50 cents per hour.

Like my previous executive position, I was required to keep the food warehouse clean and in order and it was a tough job. One of my tasks was to help the butcher make hamburger or slice lunchmeat.

In the warehouse was a large barrel of dill pickles and I had to keep filling the butcher's pan with dill pickles when it was empty. Now these pickles were very delicious and when I was cleaning the warehouse, I used to reach in and grab a pickle and eat. If I heard someone coming I would throw the pickle back into the barrel (not a sanitary thing to do).

I worked there for about a year when a new owner took over the store from Ray Mathis. The new owner recognized my executive ability and kept me on. As the summer wore on I did my usual warehouse chores always relying on the pickle barrel when I was in need of a snack.

One day the butcher asked me to go out to the warehouse and fill the pan with pickles and you guessed it...Grandpa Bigdog was in real trouble. Every time he reached into the barrel he came up with a partially chewed dill pickle. You see over the summer I had eaten quite a few pickles halfway and never kept track of the level in the barrel. GBD finally found enough pickles to fill the tray.

Lucky for GBD summer was over and I went back to school and had to quit my job.
I wonder what that butcher did when he found a barrel loaded with half eaten dill pickles?

LOOK...A RACCOON

When your Daddy was in high school he played in the Youth Symphony at Indiana University. Aunt Irene also played in the symphony and she too played the violin.

So every Saturday morning, Grandma Bigdog and Grandpa Bigdog used to take them to the University for rehearsal. After dropping them off, Grandma Bigdog and Grandpa Bigdog would go on to the Farmer's market to shop and to meet friends.

Grandpa drove an old beetle bug and your Daddy and Aunt Irene sat in the back seat with their violins. As usual, we were always late and had to hurry to get to the rehearsal on time.

One Saturday morning as we were driving down Ironwood Drive, Grandma Bigdog shouted to Grandpa Bigdog. "Look there is a raccoon in the yard over there". Well, Grandpa had already driven past the road where she saw the raccoon and were waiting at a stoplight. Grandma Bigdog told Grandpa Bigdog to go back to look at the raccoon which was sitting in the front yard of a home.

Since it was late Grandpa did not want to go back, but turned around and went back to see the creature.

Well, after waiting at two stoplights and going back Grandpa Bigdog finally drove by the house to see the...Oooops.

Well, it was not a raccoon, but a small dogwood stump that looked like a raccoon.

Well, we finally got to the rehearsal, but were late because of the raccoon or was it a stump?

ROTTEN RODNEY'S CAR

When Grandpa Bigdog was going to high school he lived in Campbell, California. World War II was on and there was gasoline rationing as well as other items like food and sugar. Now people who had automobiles could only get a certain amount of gas for the month and when that was used, you would have to park the car till the next month's ration card arrived in the mail. One of Grandpa Bigdog's friends was Bob Garcia who lived on Central Avenue. Bob's father operated a plumbing shop and Bob was a living example of a "Rotten Rodney", since he had creative ways to get into trouble.

Bob had an old Model A Ford sedan and he used to take us for a ride around Campbell. One of the unique features of a Model A is that once the engine got hot, it would burn kerosene and the car would still operate. Depending on how the choke was set it would burn with little smoke or if you turned the choke full right it would put out a smoke screen like a destroyer hiding its aircraft carrier.

One evening Rotten Rodney came by GBD's house with Frank Smith and Merrill Grim and wanted to know if GBD wanted a ride. Bob had just got two gallons of gas and started his Model A and then poured a few gallons of kerosene in the tank to keep it running.

So GBD got in and off we went riding up the dry creek bed of the Los Gatos Creek having a great time. After wearing out the gravel roads in the creek bed, Rotten Rodney headed down to Dry Creek Road making a lot of noise in the process. When we finally swung around to Willow Glen Way RR stopped at a stop sign. There was a city bus behind us and Bob turned the choke all the way to the right and gunned the engine. Huge clouds of white smoke billowed out the back. When Bob started off again we looked back to see the bus completely covered in white smoke.

Unfortunately, when we got home our clothes reeked of kerosene and we had to have them washed which didn't make Great Grandma Olivia too happy.

RUN WALLY RUN

Many years ago, Uncle Wally bought an old Model T Ford car. The model T had several features that you had to learn to operate the car. There were three spoon shaped pedals under the steering wheel. The left pedal had three positions. When the left pedal was out the car would be in high gear. When the pedal was press half way in, the car was in neutral and when pressed all the way in, it was in low gear. In order to go backward, the driver pressed the left pedal halfway in and then pressed on the middle pedal and the car would go in the reverse direction. The right pedal was used to apply brakes. Another feature was the emergency brake, which when pulled back would move the left pedal to the neutral position so the car would not go forward.

Well Uncle Wally's emergency brake would not stay locked, so he cut a piece of wood to hold the brake in place when he had to crank the engine to start the car. There was a crank at the front of the car and Uncle Wally would get in front of the car and turn the crank to start the engine.

One day, Uncle Wally had parked his Model T in Auntie Annie's yard under the coconut trees to do some work on the car. When he got ready to start the car, he put the wood in place and began to crank the car. As the engine started with a lot of noise and vibration, the wood piece came off and the car began to chase Uncle Wally through the coconut trees. The car finally hit a coconut tree and stopped, while Uncle Wally was running for his life…Run Wally Run…see Wally Run.

SECRET CODE

When Grandpa Big Dog was growing up, he lived in Honolulu. We had moved a few times and from what I could remember I had lived on Emma Street near the Buddhist Temple. From there I remember moving to Awaiolimu Street near Mrs. Cosme. From there we moved up the street further to a house with 3 bedrooms.

At Christmas time GBD's father used to come home and spend the holidays with us. Greatgrandpa was an indigent who lived in a hospital and Dr. Mossman would arrange for him to come home at Christmas that made us all very happy.

After a while we moved to another house in back of that house since the landlord wanted the house for his son-in-law.

After Greatgrandpa died we moved to 1822A Boyd Lane. Since we were on welfare, we couldn't have a radio or we would lose our benefit. Cousin Peter Carvalho (Double Rope's son) bought us a small table radio, which we would hide when the caseworker showed up.

Uncle Paul and I used to listen to a lot of radio shows...I Love a Mystery, Lone Ranger and Little Orphan Annie.

Little Orphan Annie was a young girl with a very rich father and she got into and out a lot of adventures, which were very exciting. During the middle of the show, the announcer would give out a secret code and anyone who had a secret ring could determine what the code was.

GBD did not have secret ring because it required several labels to be sent in to somewhere in the United States.

Well, one day GBD collected 3 labels and a 3-cent stamp and mailed in the labels. Now came the long wait for the ring with the secret code.

After about six weeks the ring came and GBD was so proud and couldn't wait to use it.

One day Uncle Paul and GBD listened to Little Orphan Annie with a pencil and paper eagerly waiting for the secret code.

"Here boys and girls is the secret code", said the announcer:

15-22-1-12-20-9-14-5

We were so excited and could hardly wait for the program to end so we could find out what the secret word was. We were expecting something really important and here is what we got:

O-V-A-L-T-I-N-E

So much for secret codes and the long wait for the secret ring.

THE GIANT SLINGSHOT

SLING SHOT

When Grandpa Bigdog lived in Hawaii we were very poor. We did not have many toys, so we had to use our imagination to develop games and to make our own toys.

I have told you about Games we used to play such as marbles, stick, skate cars, and hide and seek. One of the fun toys we made was the slingshot.

In Hawaii there are many bushes such as the koa bushes which saved Uncle Paul's life when he committed suicide by running Uncle Wally's wagon off the edge of the stonewall. Well, the guava bush is one of GBD's favorite plants. This bush grows wild in Hawaii. Double Rope's dairy was covered with guava bushes and there is a very delicious fruit that you can pick from this bush. The branches of the guava bush grow into a perfect "Y" making it an excellent base for a slingshot.

Uncle Wally was a master at the slingshot. He would cut a "Y" from a guava bush then cut thin pieces of an old inner tube to produce two rings of elastic, which he cut to make two long strips of rubber. Then he took a piece of leather from an old belt to make the holder for the stones. He would then wrap the ends of the rubber band to the top of the Y and tie it with string. This is where Uncle Paul and GBD came in handy to help tie those knots.

Uncle Wally then fastens the other ends of the rubber to the leather to finish the slingshot. Now for a trial. There were many nice round stones around and Uncle Wally could practice shooting at tin cans.

Some of Uncle Wally's accomplishments include shooting at the big gong at the Buddhist Temple and the Japanese man who was lighting a fire across Pauoa Stream.

Uncle Paul and GBD also had slingshots and we used to have a lot of fun with them.

One day Uncle Wally decided to have a war with Uncle Paul and GBD. Since Uncle Wally was a real expert shot we were troubled about how to counter his skills.

Uncle Paul came up with a great idea. We would build a big slingshot and take care of Uncle Wally. So, Uncle Paul found this huge guava tree stump and we made this enormous sling shot. It was so big that we could shoot large stones. The only problem was that it was too slow.

So we set up the slingshot in the empty lot next to our house and Uncle Wally took up his position on a rock pile at the bottom of Whiting Street next to Sonny Ornelas house and the battle was on.

I would hand a big rock to Uncle Paul who would load the slingshot. We then both pulled as hard as we could and let the big rock fly. We made helmets out of coffee cans to protect our heads.

This was a futile fight. Uncle Wally could see our rocks coming, but we were afraid to raise our heads up since he could shoot a lot faster. Lucky for us we never got killed with such a foolish game. But, we did have fun anyway and that was the biggest sling shot I ever saw.

I wonder if Julius Caesar had had a weapon like this he might still be emperor.

DON'T SMOKE

When Grandpa was growing up in Honolulu he did a lot of things with his friends. One of the less desirable things we did and something you should never do is to smoke cigarettes.

Uncle Paul and I with Eddie and Walter Mederios used to look in the gutters for used cigarettes and light them and smoke them. We thought this was big stuff, but when we got home Great Grandma Olivia could smell that we were smoking, even though we would deny we were.

So how do you stop kids from smoking? Well GGO had a great idea. She did not have much schooling, but she was loaded with common sense. So she told Uncle Paul and I that if we did not smoke she would let us each buy a cigar and smoke it in the house in front of our friends on New Years Eve.

In Hawaii New Years Eve is like the Fourth of July in the states and there are many celebrations with firecrackers and rockets going off all during the night such that the street was littered with paper from the firecrackers on New Years Day.

So Uncle Paul quit picking up cigarette butts and promised not to smoke until New Years Eve. Uncle Paul and Grandpa told our friends about this big event and the word got out what a good mother we had.

New Years Eve…the Big Night.

About eight o'clock that night GGO gave Uncle Paul and Grandpa a nickel each...big money to us since we lived on welfare. By now Eddie, Walter, Willie Olivera, and a few others had gathered for the ceremony. Uncle Paul and I trekked up to Chun Ho Lee store and each bought a White Owl cigar and went back home with our disciples following us.

So Uncle Paul sat in a rocking chair and lit up his cigar. The assembled fans had eyes the size of saucers as they watched this great event and Uncle Paul as he blew big clouds of smoke all over the room.

"What a good Mother you have Paul and Tom" cried the excited chorus. All eyes were glued on Uncle Paul until the cigar was more than half consumed.

Then we went out to play, burning firecrackers, chasing each other up and down Lusitana Street and having a great time.

Later on as I ran past a darkened garage I heard: "**ooooooooooooooooooooooooooooh!**" "**ooooooooooooooooooooooooooooh!**" I went into the garage and there was Uncle Paul sick as a dog.

"Don't smoke your cigar" he pleaded with Grandpa.

Lucky for Grandpa I didn't and managed to survive. So Nicky, DON'T SMOKE!!!!

So Great Grandma Olivia taught us a good lesson.

SUICIDE

When GBD was growing up in Honolulu he lived on Awaiolimu Street in Pauoa Valley. Since our home was on the slopes of Punchbowl, the land was steep and sloped down to Pauoa Stream, a small creek flowing from Mt. Tantalus.

Our back yard ran back to a stone wall which dropped down about ten feet to the stream where there were a lot of koa trees growing there. These trees are thin, about the size of a broom handle and grow close together.

Uncle Wally raised pigeons and rabbits. He would spend his afternoons pulling weeds, pulleleis, to feed his rabbits. He also had a big, heavy wagon to load the rabbit grass. For example, he would go up to Papakulea where he could get a lot of grass, load it on his wagon, then fly down Puouwaina Drive, down to Whiting Street and home. Many times the brakes failed and he had trouble stopping the wagon.

Enter Uncle Paul.

When the wagon was idle, Uncle Paul would use the wagon to ride up and down the back yard. There were two trees in the yard, a mango on the left and a lemon on the right. So if Uncle Paul went down near the mango tree he would call that Ft. Ruger route and roar down till he reached the stone wall and turned left to avoid flying off into the koa trees. If he went right he called that route Ft. Shafter route and did the same.

One day Uncle Paul was giving GBD, Aunt Lorraine and Aunt Eva rides. Uncle Paul was a sneaky guy so he asked Aunt Eva which route she wanted. She said "Ft. Ruger" but instead he took Ft. Shafter and her dress got caught in the big wagon wheels and she fell off the wagon.

Aunt Eva was not too happy about that, but we kept riding the wagon up and down the yard.

Uncle Paul used to hog the wagon and always insisted that he would drive it down the yard.

One day we all got mad at Uncle Paul and he in turn said that he was going to commit suicide. So he got on the wagon and roared down the yard toward the stone wall, hanging onto the steering ropes of the wagon.

Instead of turning at the stone wall, Uncle Paul roared off the wall and he and the heavy wagon went flying through the air into the koa trees.

Lucky for Uncle Paul, he was unhurt, but we had a heck of time trying to lift the heavy wagon back over the stonewall. Uncle Wally was not too happy about that and told Uncle Paul he couldn't do that again.

PAUL, WALLY, LORRAINE, EVA, TOM

TAKE THE BUS

When Grandpa Bigdog lived in Honolulu the public transportation system consisted of street cars. These were electric powered cars that ran on tracks down the middle of the road. One could ride all over Honolulu by streetcar.

For example, when we had to go to Palama Settlement for medical treatment, we would go to Lusitana Street which was the end of the line in front of Chun Ho Lee's store. When the streetcar came to the end of the line, the conductor would move the controls to the other end of the car and reconnect the trolley line to the electric cable above for the return trip.

To go to Palama the streetcar would go down Lusitana Street to Emma Street then to King Street. There it would turn onto King Street then turned up Kalihi Street. When we got to School Street we got off the streetcar and walked over to Palama Settlement.

Later on the Rockefellers bought up the streetcars, tore up the tracks and replaced the streetcars with trolleys and gasoline buses to sell more gasoline. So now instead of streetcars we had small buses going up and down Lusitana Street.

Eddie Medeiros and I used to wave at the bus drivers as they went by. Eventually we got friendly with one of the drivers who let us ride the bus without having a fare. This was really great stuff.

So, after school Eddie and I would stand by the bus stop and wait for the right driver to come by. Well, our friend soon showed up and we would get on the bus and ride all over Honolulu.

This was really a lot of fun until one day Eddie and I were going down Emma Street when the bus driver saw that there was an Inspector waiting on the corner of Emma and King Streets. This could be big trouble for him.

So he dumped us off and gave us transfers. Then he continued his route down to Kakaako. That was a real bad part of town. When the bus came back to King Street we got back on and went home. That was a close shave.

One day GBD was riding a trolley with my bus driver friend. At the end of the line, the driver stopped to go to the bathroom and GBD got into the driver's seat and drove the huge trolley up the street...not a smart move, but a neat trick for a 12 year old. The bus driver was not too happy about that stunt.

At any rate, GBD and Eddie got to see a lot of Honolulu by taking the bus.

THE BICYCLE

When Grandpa was growing up, we lived in Honolulu. My oldest brother Wally had a bicycle which he used to go to Industrial Arts school, where he learned to be a machinist. After Uncle Wally finished school, he went to work at Pearl Harbor as a machinist apprentice and eventually became a master machinist.

Uncle Wally was proud of his bicycle and he parked it on the front porch and locked the crank with a combination lock while he was at work. Since Pearl Harbor was a long way from where we lived, Uncle Wally rode in a motor pool with a friend of his and two others who also worked at the Naval Yard at Pearl Harbor.

Enter Uncle Paul. Uncle Paul would like to have rode the bicycle, but couldn't because Uncle Wally told us we couldn't use his bicycle...that is why he locked the bicycle. Well, Uncle Paul was kind of a sneaky character and he spent hours trying to figure out the combination to the lock. One day, he finally figured out how to open the lock and get the bicycle out.

Uncle Paul carefully marked the position of the wheels and how the pedals were set, so he could return the bicycle to exactly the same way each day, so that Uncle Wally would never know that anyone had used his bicycle. As a result, Uncle Paul used to spend his afternoons cruising around Holy Ghost Hill and up and down Boyd and Bush lanes as well as up and down Lusitana street.

Uncle Wally usually came home from work about five o'clock in the afternoon such that Uncle Paul was always careful to make sure he had the bicycle put back and the pedals set so that no one knew the bicycle was used. Uncle Paul thought he was pretty smart to have figured this out and he hoped that Grandpa or Auntie Eva or Lorraine would not tell Uncle Wally.

Then came the day of reckoning and as all bad things must come to a just end. One afternoon, Uncle Paul was cruising up and down Lusitana

Street when up pulled a car with Uncle Wally in it. Uncle Paul rode past the car and called out, "Hi Wally…ooops", he got caught. It seemed that Uncle Wally was sent home early from the Naval Yard that day and Uncle Paul had no idea he would be home early.

That was the end of Uncle Paul and his joy riding.

So, you see many times we think we can get away with doing what we should not do, but we always get caught. I wish you could have seen the surprised look on Uncle Paul's face when he got caught.

WALLY & BIKE

THE CHOKE

After World War II, there was a great shortage of automobiles. For our country World War II started in 1941 and automobile production for civilians stopped. By the time the war ended in 1945 auto production began again, but cars were difficult to buy. As a result, older cars were in demand.

Enter super salesman Benjamin Carvalho.

Grandpa's cousin Ben was a used car salesman and he sold a 1936 Chevrolet coupe to his brother Eddie. (He should have gone to jail for selling that pile of junk, especially to his brother.) In those old cars there was a choke control and an accelerator control mounted on the dash. Well, in this junk the choke control would slowly work its way out and stall the engine. As a result, Eddie had to push the choke control in frequently, such that it became an automatic reflex for him to push the choke in.

Grandpa used to ride around with cousin Eddie and often laughed at this funny practice. Well, oneday cousin Eddie bought a new 1949 Chevrolet. He was quite proud of his new car and came by to give Grandpa a ride. Well, what do you know…cousin Eddie still had the habit of pushing the choke in and every few minutes you could see him reaching up to the dash board to press in the light switch in the place where the old choke used to be.

I guess old habits are hard to break.

THE DUET

When Grandpa Bigdog was in high school he had a friend name Albert Evans. Al's father had an apricot ranch and one day when I was there, Al showed GBD his tenor sax. Well GBD knew nothing about music, so I asked him how he could read music. So he loaned me his saxophone and some music and I went home and started learning to play.

GBD enrolled in Beginning Band when I was a junior and began to study music. Well, when Mrs. Evans found out that Al had loaned me the sax she was furious and demanded I return it. She was right since it was an expensive instrument. So GBD bought an alto sax and continued till I could play pretty well.

Another good friend of GBD was Mac Martin. Mac was first trumpet in the band and a very good musician. Toward the end of the spring semester, Mac bought an alto sax and began to learn how to play it.

Soon summer was upon us and we joined a summer youth group. One of the functions the group planned was to have a talent show for the public. GBD thought it was a good idea, but Mac was a bit reluctant. At any rate we began rehearsing a saxophone duet. We decided to do "Always" and "Jumping at the Woodside". In addition, we enlisted Marceline Benesch to accompany us on the piano. Well Marceline was an accomplished pianist and agreed to help us.

Well the big night came and a lot of the parents were at hand. The first up was Ledean Garrison. He had no accompanist and sang, "Saturday Night is the Loneliest Night of the Week". Then came the piece de resistance: Mac Martin and the Kingfish [Grandpa Bigdog].

Here we go…I'll be loving you Al…**squeeeeeeeeeeeeeeeeek**. [GBD's reed split and gave the loud squeak.] Well, Mac began to laugh, while GBD was trying to keep a straight face, Marceline gave up on us and Mac began to HO HO HO so bad that he couldn't blow the sax. Meanwhile, the parents were trying to be kind, but finally gave up and burst into laughter…the rest was like a Laurel and Hardly comedy, since GBD was trying so hard to be professional and Mac couldn't control his laughter.

As a result we never got to be famous due to sinus trouble…nobody would sign us up.

MAC MARTIN

THE MUMMY'S TOMB

When Grandpa Bigdog was growing up in Honolulu he lived near Punchbowl with Uncle Paul and Uncle Wally, Aunts Eva and Lorraine and our mother Great Grandma Olivia.

We lived on Awaiolimu Street near those famous graveyards. While growing up, one of the big deals was to go to the movies. Unfortunately, the movies cost ten cents and we did not have that kind of money. We used to envy the rich kids who could go to the movies. [Rich to us was anyone who could afford to go to the movies or to buy a bag of semoi or cracked seed].

As we grew older we became more affluent. GBD obtained an executive position with Mrs. Cosme, a very kind lady who lived nearby and used to baby sit Aunt Lorraine. She used to pay me ten cents on Saturday to mow her lawn. This was done with a reel mower that had to be pushed. In spite of that, GBD was able to get the job done and pick up my big pay.

Well, this was enough money for us to go to the movies. Meanwhile, Uncle Paul found odd jobs and was able to acquire ten cents, so every Saturday afternoon we would head off for the Roosevelt Theater in downtown Honolulu.

To get to the theater we walked down Awaiolimu Street to Lusitana Street then cut through the Buddhist Temple over to Fort Street past the Queen's Theater, then over to the Roosevelt Theater.

The usual fare was a cowboy picture featuring Gene Autry, Roy Rodgers, Ken Maynard, The Three Musketeers or Hopalong Cassidy. There was also a serial that was a must for all kids to see. Some of these were Dick Tracy, Tarzan, Mala and Flash Gordon.

One day GBD and Uncle Paul went to our usual Saturday movie and the picture they were showing was "The Mummy's Tomb" with Lon Chaney and George Zukor.

We were taken by surprise and scared out of our wits. When the movie ended, Uncle Paul got a great idea.

"Let's go hide in the bathroom and see the movie again," He said.

Well, we did just that and watched the movie again getting more scared with each showing.

When the movie ended we stepped out into the street and low and behold, the sun was setting and it was getting dark. So we hurried up the street past the Queen's Theater stopping at each alley to peek around the corner to see if the mummy was coming after us. When we finally got to the Buddhist Temple, it was now dark and as we past the porch the priest rang the large bell...**GOOOOONNNNG!!** and scarred the wits out of us. We ran for our lives and did not stop running till we got home.

That's what we got by cheating on the movie. Watch out for the mummy!!

THE SEWER COVER

When Grandpa was growing up in Honolulu, he used to spend a lot of his time riding a bicycle. By now, Uncle Wally's famous bike was used a lot by Uncle Paul and Grandpa.

Grandpa's best friend is Eddie Mederios and he and Grandpa used to spend a lot of hours riding our bikes. We used to like to ride up steep hills, like Holy Ghost Hill and glide down at high speed.

Eddie had a very special bike. It had knee action, that is, the front fork was suspended from a large spring and it acted like a shock absorber making riding over bumps a lot smoother and Eddie's bike was the envy of the rest of the kids. Eddie used to like to show off with the knee action and could jump curves and show off his fancy bike.

One day after school Eddie and I went riding up and down Lusitana street, where Eddie lived. After wearing out that street, we decided to do some exploring some other hilly streets so we went down Kuakini Street over to Nuuanu Street and Kawanakakoa School then up Nuuanu Street toward the Pali. Near Our Lady of Peace school there was a steep hill leading past a graveyard and Iolani school.

So Eddie and I started up the hill and rode up quite a ways because the ride down would be fast and smooth sailing. When we got up as far as we wanted to go we turned around and began racing down the hill. Eddie was faster than Grandpa and he was really going fast.

Eddie decided it was time to show off so he let go of the handlebars and steered the bike by balancing his weight from one side to another.

Grandpa decided to do the same and here were two pupuli kids racing down Nuuanu Street having the time of their lives…but not for long!

You see as Eddie was heading down the steepest part of the street he saw two sewer covers in the middle of the street. Eddie being a daring guy decided to steer the bike between the two sewer covers and really show off and show off he did.

As Eddie swung his body to the right to miss the first sewer cover the front wheel of his bike jammed and collapsed. Because of the knee action, the seat of the bike came up and hit Eddie in the seat propelling him into space. (I think Eddie was the first space man).

Poor Eddie went sprawling onto the gravel road and scraped his arms, forehead and shoulders…the bike was smashed. The first thing Eddie did was to pick up the bike to check if the back wheel could still turn.

We carried the injured bike home and poor Eddie got bandaged up and smeared with Mercurichrome which was an all purpose medicine. For the next few weeks Eddie looked like he had fallen off a cliff.

So Nicky, watch out for sewer covers and don't show off on your bike.

THREE GALLONS

When Grandpa Bigdog started college, he got a job as a movie projectionist in a Mexican theater. This was the CINEMA in Mt. View, California and about 10 miles from where GBD lived.

Since GBD just graduated from high school, he did not have an automobile and in order to take that job, GBD had to buy a car. This was in 1946 and new cars were very expensive and most people had used cars, since during World War II they stopped making automobiles.

The Business Agent of the union knew a friend who ran a gas station and he told me that his friend had a good car for sale. So GBD went to look at the car...a blue 1934 Ford sedan. This car was selling for $585 and that was all the money GBD had in his bank account, but he bought this car.

One of the first problems GBD encountered was that the gas gauge did not work, so there was no way of telling how far it would go without running out of gas.

Now in those days, gas stations would fill your tank, wash the windshield, check the oil and water level and the air pressure in the tires...try to get that today!!

GBD lived in Campbell and I would have to drive 5 miles to San Jose to college. After school I drove home, then to Mt. View and then back home.

So what GBD did was after dinner he would drive to Jones Shell Station on Winchester Avenue and ask for three gallons of gas. This cost sixty cents and would keep me running until I got back to the station on the next night. So every day GBD had to come up with sixty cents to cover my gas cost.

After a while the station attendants would see me coming and they wouldn't even ask me what I needed, they would just give GBD 3 gallons of gas and GBD would roar off in his blue equipage.

This car was a real pile of junk and that will be another story for next time. Remind GBD to write about that car and all the trouble he had with it. That series could be as long as the Grave Yard Tales.

So if you ever see GBD drive into a gas station you will know that he came in for:

THREE GALLONS

TRAIN'S COMING

When Grandpa was in high school, he lived in Campbell, California near the Southern Pacific Railroad. In other words, we lived on the other side of the tracks. Every morning a large passenger train would come by on its way to Los Gatos and it would return to San Jose in the evening. The train crossed Campbell Avenue near Grandpa's house.

Enter Jack Vitale!

He had a 1938 Dodge sedan and he would take us for a ride around town. One of Jack's stunts was to try to drive his car down the railroad tracks. He would start where the railroad crossed Campbell Avenue and carefully maneuver his car over the rails and drive down the track for a few hundred feet with the gang all cheering him along. Each time he tried this, he got a bit bolder and drove further down the track. One day he picked up a few friends and decided to see how far he could go without his tires falling off the rails. The next drive off road from Campbell Avenue was Hamilton Avenue, one mile away and the tracks were lined with steep slopes on each side.

At any rate, Jack was off on his new adventure, with a carload of friends. He was able to maneuver his carload of pals and drive on until…you guessed it…a train came down the track right at Jack and his car. Lucky for Jack the train was a switch engine carrying some boxcars and the train stopped. The engineer was laughing at Jack and began to back the train so that Jack and his now scared friends could reach Hamilton Avenue and safety.

That was the last time Jack got onto the tracks.

WRONG CAR

When Grandpa Bigdog was a young man, he lived in Campbell, California. Great Grandma Olivia had a cousin Sophie and they were good friends. Cousin Sophie had a big Buick sedan and used to take Great Grandma Olivia shopping.

Well, one day Great Grandma Olivia and cousin Sophie went to San Jose to shop and parked in a parking lot. Great Grandma Olivia went one way and cousin Sophie went the other, but agreed to meet in Sophie's car. Great Grandma Olivia got back early and sat in the car waiting for Sophie. Soon a couple approached the car. Great Grandma Olivia rolled down the window see what they wanted and they told her...whoops...she was sitting in the wrong car.

You see, Great Grandma Olivia did not know the difference between cars.

Enter Grandma Bigdog. She too doesn't know about cars. Years ago, Grandpa took her to the dime store. We just bought a new 1965 Chevrolet and parked in front of the store. As we left the store, Grandma Bigdog headed for another white car parked in front of the store and got into the car, while Grandpa went on and sat in our own car. Soon Grandpa began to wave at Grandma Bigdog who was wondering where I was. WHOA!!! When she realized she was in the wrong car, she got out quickly and came to our car. She was not too happy with Grandpa, but she seemed to inherit the same talent as Great Grandma Olivia.

GREAT GRANDMA OLIVIA

68

RELIGIOUS

THOMAS J. MIRANDA

HELP WANTED - APPLY ABOVE

Have you ever passed a store window and seen a sign HELP WANTED - APPLY WITHIN? Did you ever stop to think of the reasoning behind that sign? Well, the person who placed the sign obviously could not accomplish his task alone or could do it more effectively if he or she had additional help. Therefore, by seeking and paying for help, a person is able to satisfy a particular need.

The need for help is all around us. We become so dependent upon others ever since our birth, that it is a natural tendency to seek help at the first sign of a problem, need or difficulty.

But, what about the quality of help? Assume that sign was for a dishwasher in a restaurant. The help obtained may vary from a highly dedicated, sincere, hard worker to that of a careless, unmotivated and incompetent person. Mistakes will always be made - regardless of the help whether it is a dishwasher, or a highly trained corporate executive, scientist, engineer, or toolmaker. In addition, regardless of the quality of the worker, payment or reward of some kind goes hand in hand with the job. We have numerous examples today of highly paid people doing jobs at the lowest ebb of their potential. If their work is not of good quality they, in many cases, are not brought to task for it, although they must be paid regardless. In summary then, to get help you must seek it, pay for it and never be sure you will obtain the quality of help you may desire.

I am reminded of a story of a man who was stalled on the highway and asked another motorist for a push. He also cautioned the motorist that since he had an automatic transmission, he would have to be pushed at 35 miles per hour to get started. Much to his dismay he looked up into his rear view mirror to see his `help' coming at his stalled car at 35 miles per hour!!

To get help we apply within, and around us. But, where can we get help which is perfect, willing, high quality, error free and absolutely without cost? THAT IS A MYTH!!

Not so! Instead of applying within, we should apply above. The Lord Jesus Christ is the perfect help that we can call upon for our every need. His help is perfect, free, and willing. Perhaps our biggest problem, though, is that instead of going to Him when we first need help, we always consider Him as a court of last resort—when all else fails, then pray quickly and hope that He will come to your aid. This is similar to an employer who goes out and hires the most unqualified people to do a job, but after numerous failures, finally in desperation, turns to skilled, tried workers to accomplish a task.

For help in need, Jesus is always there, ready night and day, storm or fair weather, eager and willing to help. Christians must learn to go to Him first before they turn to others for help. He can act like the shop steward, who either assigns someone to assist us, or He may turn circumstances about to help you.

What do we do to have such a great partner?

The simple answer is—NOTHING! That is right—NOTHING!

We should do nothing that will cause us to be alienated from His presence. That is our thoughts, deeds and actions must fit His purpose for us. Sin has no place in His or our goals, and is the biggest stumbling block that keeps Him from opening the door to answer our plea for help.

If you don't believe that this is true we can provide proof from the Master's own words in the Sermon on the Mount—"Ask and you shall receive, seek and you shall find, knock and it shall be opened unto you." (Matt 7:7). He is also eager for us to seek Him out. (Matt 11:28)

Here is a simple test. The next time you have a problem, turn first quickly to Him and seek His help. This could be from simply looking for a parking place on a crowded street to a more serious problem. But, whatever, got to Him first! You see, He cares for you (1 Pet 5-7), and is eager to help you and knows what you need even before you ask (Matt 6:8).

I remember seeing a sign on the inside rear door of a bread truck which read: "IT'S YOURS FOR THE ASKING—BUT YOU MUST ASK." It is the same with God, help is yours for the asking—but you must ask.

And, whatever you do, don't forget to thank Him. Remember the Samaritan leper who returned to give thanks. Human nature being what it is we forget to thank Him, but fortunate for us, He has a forgiving heart. Remember also, that when God answers prayer be careful—He usually overdoes it—your cup will surely run over. (Ps 23: 5).

So, when you need help, "APPLY ABOVE."

ALONE

Rear Admiral Richard E. Byrd wrote a book entitled "Alone" in which he described his mission to the Antarctic continent. He chose to spend a dark winter alone in that forbidden land with extreme conditions of cold and utter loneliness. As I read the book many years ago, I could not help becoming very distressed. His hardships grew on you as you passed through the pages. The only relief the reader can receive, is putting the book down then trying to get warm.

Perhaps the most difficult part of his ordeal was the utter loneliness he experienced. One wonders about how he could have maintained his sanity during that long winter. Byrd had no one to talk to...his only communication was the simple radio transmissions he made to his men far away. Being alone Byrd nearly succumbed to carbon monoxide poisoning.

Being alone is a real problem today. As people reach old age, they become more and more alone as younger people, busier with their own climb up the ladder of life have less time for them. A person can also be alone in a number of other ways. When someone faces a severe problem, many times that person must do so alone, either due to the nature of the problem or the lack of concern others may have, intentional or otherwise, for their problem. Then there is the famous cartoon in which an individual is surrounded by thousands of people who cries out that he is "all alone". A person can also be alone when tragedy strikes, like losing a loved one.

Perhaps the greatest example of being alone, was when Jesus endured the cross and was rejected by the Father. The bible tells us that the worst a sinner can receive is condemnation to hell where hell fire consumes the evil spirits. I also heard a more vivid and terrifying view of hell, that being total darkness, utter terror and fear and the knowledge that one would never see the face of Jesus. This is far worse than any description of hell I have ever encountered. Sometimes being alone is a good thing; allowing one to sort out things mentally or solving a problem. Jesus did this many times; he sought to be alone where he could pray to obtain strength to resolve the many problems he surely encountered. At times, one cannot be alone as intruders tend to interrupt. Jesus, in the desert, was alone until Satan decided to put Him to the test. For our sake He won that contest. While being alone has its perils and benefits, we should realize that we are really not alone.

No matter what we do we always have Jesus at our side. It's like having a personal consultant, one who is all powerful, at your side at all times. No matter what we do He is always there. The most important aspect of this truth is that He will be with us when we need Him most...at our departure.

No matter who you are or whom you know, there will be no one to go with you on that last journey. Since He will be your tour guide on the most important journey you will ever take, wouldn't it be a good idea to get to know Him and to serve Him better.

AMY'S BIG DAY
(To Julie)

Amy got up early this morning because she heard a pair of mourning doves outside her window. She looked out her window and saw the birds pecking at seeds on the ground and singing a welcome to the new day. In the distance, across the sagebrush, she could see the brown hills towering up to the desert sky. Small clouds were forming in the sky that would become large billowing puffs during the day. It was another day in the desert as spring hastened into summer.

"It's time to get up, Amy", her mother called as she came into her room.

Amy threw her arms around her mother and hugged her. Her mother helped her to dress and eased her into her wheel chair. Amy was crippled and could not walk, so she spent her day in the wheel chair. Her mother couldn't afford to take her to a doctor, but Amy was content with her life, since she could spend a lot of time on the back porch of her little house and watch the birds and animals.

It was lonely in the desert and Amy had no human friends or even a doll to play with. She did however, have some good friends in the animals and birds. Squirrels, rabbits and birds would gather at her doorstep and she would talk to them and feed them. Amy used to have fun with the squirrels by tying a piece of bread to a string and tossing it onto the sand. As one of the squirrels would reach for the bread she would pull the string and the squirrel would jump back startled. But, he would come back again until he was on the porch. In this way, Amy could have many of her squirrel friends close to her wheel chair.

Amy's back porch faced the railroad tracks and the highlight of her day was when the streamliner would come past the house. As the day wore on Amy's excitement grew as she kept a sharp ear tuned to the West. Several times she thought she could hear a whistle. Finally, in the distance she saw a wisp of smoke appear on the horizon. Slowly, the little speck on the track grew larger as the huge locomotive bore down the track at high speed. As the train neared her house the squirrels scurried away and the birds flew away. Just then the whistle blew; for the engineer always blew the whistle as he came near Amy's house. As the train roared by Amy waved to the train. The engineer and the fireman waved back and rang the bell. Amy tried to read the names on the cars as the colorful passenger cars whisked by. Finally, the club car signaled the end of the train; Amy saw the conductor and porter standing and waving from the back of the train. Amy's eyes were fixed on the train until it disappeared into the eastern desert.

This was Amy's big event of the day.

After the noise settled down, the animals and birds slowly returned. Soon it was time for lunch and Amy's mother wheeled her into the house. During the afternoon, the sun beat down on the desert and Amy would remain indoors, until it cooled off at night. Her animal friends would be gone also.

One morning Amy sat out on the porch as usual looking for her animal friends and glancing down the railroad track to watch for her train. After a while, she saw a wisp of smoke on the horizon. Slowly the giant locomotive loomed larger on the track. She heard the familiar whistle that always alerted her. As she started to wave, she noticed something unusual—the train was slowing down! The big bell on the locomotive was ringing and she could hear the brakes grinding the huge engine to a halt—right in front of her. Amy was frightened—she did not know what to do.

The engineer, fireman and conductor were climbing down from the engine. The conductor was carrying a large doll. The engineer had a box of candy and a bear and the fireman carried flowers and a box of candy.

Amy was speechless.

The conductor asked her name and said "My name is Ed Roberts and I have a doll for you".

Amy never had a doll and hugged the doll tightly. The engineer gave her the candy and the fireman the flowers and bear. Just then, her mother appeared with another man. He was the railroad agent, who explained to Amy that the train crew had asked permission to stop the train so they could meet Amy. You see, the train crew also looked forward to greeting Amy every day. Finally, they carried Amy to the engine so she could see what it looked like. They let her ring the big bell and blow the whistle. At last they returned Amy to her wheel chair and wished her goodbye. The big engine's wheels started to turn and they were off. Amy sat for a long time looking after the train. Then she looked at her doll and cried—she was so happy.

Meanwhile, the conductor was stopped by a passenger asking him why the train had stopped in the middle of the desert. When the conductor told him the story, the passenger who was a doctor, asked for Amy's name and said that he wanted to help her. The doctor arranged for Amy to have an operation to correct her crippled condition. Soon, Amy could walk again, but she never forgot her friends and rushed out of the house each day to wave to the train and to the wonderful people who cared.

AMY GOT LOST

Amy lived near a large forest. Her home overlooked a beautiful meadow, which in the spring was alive with color as many beautiful flowers bloomed. There were all colors…red, blue, orange, yellow, such that it was like the colors of the rainbow.

A small stream flowed through the meadow and Amy would go there often to watch the little fish in the stream. She would also collect flowers and take them home to her mother.

Just behind the meadow was a large forest with tall trees. Her mother told her never to go into the forest alone, because there were bears and wolves in the forest.

One day, as Amy was playing in the meadow, she saw a beautiful blue bird and decided to catch it. The little bird flew away and waited for Amy to come closer. It seemed like a game, but as she kept following the bird, she soon found herself deep into the forest!!!

After awhile Amy realized that she was lost and did not know how to find her way back home. She sat down and began to cry. After a while, she looked up and saw a pair of yellow eyes staring at her.

IT WAS A WOLF!!!!.

Amy was frightened and did not know what to do but to just look at the wolf. The wolf came close to Amy then walked away, stopped and turned around to look back at Amy. The wolf did this a few times, as if she wanted Amy to follow her. Amy began to follow the wolf and soon came to the edge of the meadow, where she could see her home. She ran toward home. When she got home she looked back at the meadow and saw the wolf turning away to go back to the forest. Just then four little wolves came up to her; these were her babies and she must have known that little Amy was lost and needed help to get home again.

ANGEL FOR A DAY

How would you like to be an angel for a day?

The Bible cites the existence of and actions of angels in numerous books. The earliest was the angel who expelled Adam and Eve from the garden, the angels visiting Abraham, feeding Elias, rescuing Daniel and announcing to Mary that she was a chosen vessel of God. Angels, therefore, are messengers of God who carry out His orders, protect His chosen ones and serve to herd sinners for their final judgment. Angels can be divided into two categories - spirits and mortal. There are also good angels and evil angels; the latter belonging to the realm of Satan and marked for destruction at the end of the ages.

An excellent book was written by Billy Graham entitled "Angels" in which he describes in vivid detail some of the real life experiences in which people have witnessed the presence of angels. It would not be too far fetched to believe that there are many human angels about, though they are not recognized as such and do not have the attributes normally associated with angels, that is, being in the presence of God. For humans, the presence of God would be unbearable here on earth, but enjoyable after death. We can experience the presence of God when we are in a state of grace and free to give ourselves wholly to God. Then the peace of God lives in us.

Coming back to angels, however, have you ever thought of being used by God to perform the function of an angel? With all the prayer requests, which flood God each day, it would be overwhelming for Him to answer each in person (though not impossible for Him). But, could you imagine what would happen if God would appear to humans in response to our needs? There would probably be either a dramatic rise in coronaries or total disbelief (remember how Moses doubted who He was). So to solve this problem, I believe that God uses people to carry out the necessary physical deeds for which we pray.

Think about it.

Have you ever had someone appear out of nowhere when you were in need and solved a problem for you? Have you ever had circumstances twisted in such a way that you have been used to carry out a mission for God in helping someone in need?

I recall an incident when I was scheduled to return on an early afternoon flight from Chicago and the flight was cancelled due to a snowstorm. I tried to rent an automobile, but none was available, I couldn't get a bus nor a train to South Bend so I waited from two in the afternoon until the 5:30 flight; this too was cancelled! Finally, I got on a 7:30 flight, which was delayed until 8:15 waiting for a late plane from Salt Lake City.

Finally, the weary passengers clambered aboard; one sitting next to me in the middle seat. I paid no attention to the passenger as I was reading some New Testament material when she asked me if I was a minister. She was a nun who told me that she had started out from Fresno, California at six that morning and missed her connection due to bad weather. She also mentioned that she had no ride to St. Mary's College since her flight was so late. I suggested that I could take her home since I passed near there. As it happened, this sister had been a graduate student at Notre Dame while I was there, but in another research group.

After seeing sister safely to her residence hall, I then realized why I was not able to get a flight home and was required to `cool my heels' all day long. You see, God had more important things in mind. He had to see that His sister would be taken care of when she arrived in South Bend and He provided transportation for her. So, if you are inconvenienced sometime, or have a hunch that you should do some good for someone, just remember; **you may be an angel for a day!!**

BLUE

Sir Isaac Newton made an interesting discovery when he noticed a tiny beam of light shining through a small opening in a wall. He placed a prism in the path of the light and found to his amazement that the prism had split white light into a whole array of colour ranging from violet to red. While most colors are beautiful, blue seems to be special. This could be because blue appears in so many places in nature. For example, the sky, and the ocean are blue. The reason for the blue in the sky is that light is scattered in air, reflecting the shorter blue wavelengths. The ocean shows many shades of blue.

Off the coast of Hawaii, the ocean is a very deep blue reflecting the depth of the ocean just off that island. Many flowers have shades of blue. One of my favorites is the chicory flower. This plant grows along the roadsides in Indiana and Michigan on the worst soil under dry, hot conditions. Yet, in the early morning, this soft blue flower, with a golden center, appears to greet each morning and lends a certain encouragement to anyone willing to look and reflect upon its beauty.

I used to travel an hour each way to work for over 22 years, and one of the highlights of my summer treks was to see these beautiful flowers. Chicory flowers are a member of the sunflower family and tend to follow the sun in its race across the sky. Later in the day, they fold up as if to wait for another opportunity to greet a new day. These flowers also allow one to reflect on the course of our own lives and what is going on in the world today. Since these flowers grow along the roadside, highway mowers frequently cut them down. In spite of this, they soon return to their full glory. This could be a good lesson for Christians, who meet so many cut downs, but must learn to bounce back to give glory to God.

I also like to think of the soft blue of these flowers in terms of a heavenly blue, which is depicted in artwork concerning the Mother of God. In these paintings, she is shown to wear a soft blue sash very similar to the color of these beautiful flowers. She too, must appreciate the beautiful blue shades that God has spread throughout His Kingdom.

THE LITTLE BUNNY

(To Julie)

Once upon a time, long, long ago, there lived a little brown bunny. He had long ears and a big bushy tail. His mother called him Fluffy. He lived in a hole on the side of a hill with his brothers and sisters. When he was little, he spent a lot of time in the nest that his mother had made from soft grass and fur. Now and then he would wander out of the nest to a bright light at one end of his little home, but his mother would urge him back to the nest.

As he grew older, his mother warned him not to go out of the nest without her or his father.

"You must be careful of wolves and eagles" his mother warned.

She told him how some careless bunnies had been carried off by wolves and eagles. So, during the day, she told him to stay in the nest until the light went away. Then, under cover of darkness, his mother would lead the little bunnies out to eat the cool, sweet grasses that grew on the hillside. At any sign of danger, he and his brothers and sisters would scurry back to the safety of their little home.

As little Fluffy grew older, his mother would let he and his little brothers and sisters go out to the light at the end of their home. As he stepped out, he was surprised to see how bright and beautiful it was. He looked at the olive trees, tall cedars, and little cactus flowers. He saw many beautiful flowers and berries. As he looked around, he saw a funny animal looking at him. He had a long, curved tail and grey fur. Fluffy had never seen such an animal.

"What kind of an animal are you?" he asked. "Oh" said the little ball of fur, "I am a squirrel and my name is Henry".

Fluffy and Henry became good friends. Henry would climb trees and tell Fluffy of all he could see from on high. Fluffy and Henry also became friendly with the birds. There were gold finches, red cardinals, sparrows, hummingbirds, woodpeckers and robins. The birds liked Fluffy and would sing songs for him and also sound an alarm if a wolf or eagle were about.

Fluffy's mother would not let him wander far from the nest, even though there seemed to be better grass further from home. Toward evening, he would sit by the entrance to his home and watch the sunset. The birds would say goodnight and fly into the trees. Henry would climb a tree to his little house. As it grew darker, the stillness of the evening air would be broken with the sound of a cricket, then a tree toad until the whole night stillness would be drowned out by a symphony of sounds.

One evening as Fluffy was sitting outside his house, something unusual happened. He noticed the birds and all the animals hurrying over to a distant hill. They came from all directions; foxes, squirrels, deer, rabbits, field mice, chipmunks, donkeys and all you could name. They seemed to be in a hurry! Fluffy tried to find out where they were going, but they were all too busy to stop and chat with him. Finally, he asked his mother if he could go, but she refused. He did not want to disobey his mother. How he wanted to know what that was all about. Finally, he became tired and went to bed.

Several nights later, the same thing happened again. This time, even Henry went along, but again his mother would not let him go, even though he begged her. The next day Henry came by and Fluffy asked him what he saw; was there any danger?

"We went to see the King" Henry replied as he scurried up a tree. Fluffy also wanted to see the King so he told his mother about what Henry said. There was now a lot of talk in the animal community about this. Fluffy's mother went to visit Henry's mother, who had also gone to see the King.

So the next evening, Fluffy and his whole family decided to go to see the King over beyond the distant hill. Fluffy spent the afternoon cleaning his fur and washing his face. Fluffy was so excited as he hopped over the grass to the hill for he had never seen a King. As he approached the hill, he saw that it was a garden surrounded by olive trees. He stopped suddenly. Just before him stood a large rock and all the animals were gathered around the rock in a big semi-circle. The birds sat in the branches that hung low over the rock. Some of them had brought flowers for the King. But, there was no King. Fluffy sat down and looked around; the other animals were very quiet.

Fluffy was disappointed. He came so far just to see a rock - where was the King? He noticed a tired man in a grey robe walking up the hillside, obviously a gardener, but no King. After a while, the gardener came to and sat upon the rock.

The animals were delighted!

"Who's that?" he asked Henry.

"Why, it's the King!" Henry replied.

Just then, the birds started singing. Those who had brought flowers flew down from the olive branches and placed them at his feet. The King smiled and appeared to understand the animals. They watched him for a long time and the garden grew so peaceful. Fluffy then understood why all the animals came to see the King. He was overjoyed! Finally, a large deer turned away and as if it were a signal, the animals bid farewell and left for their homes.

After this, Fluffy would go to see the King whenever the animals came by. But, one day, he noticed that the animals were going to see the King but were very sad. Fluffy joined them, but as he reached the garden, he noticed that the King was not sitting on the rock, but was kneeling beside it. He was in agony; His face dripped with sweat and blood and He was very sad.

The animals were also crying! The big deer had tears running down his face and the birds did not sing. Fluffy was also sad. After a while, the animals were startled to see an angel standing by the King. They did not know what to make of this.

Suddenly, they heard noises as a large group of men bearing torches and carrying spears came toward the garden. The animals fled in fright.

This was was indeed a sad day!

After that day, the animals never went to see the King again.

HEY CULLIGAN MAN

After World War II, the American public became beneficiary of the tremendous technological advances derived from the Manhattan Project. While most people associate that project with the Atomic Bomb, there were many very significant developments that were made during the life of the Manhattan Project. Some examples include synthetic rubber, detergents and ion exchange resins. The last spawned a large consumer (and Industrial) market for water softeners. Soon, salesmen were combing the country selling water softeners and clever advertising developed to push this remarkable new product.

One of the most famous became the Culligan Company with their clever radio and TV commercials explaining to a confused lady that her water contained rocks and that with a Culligan unit, these rocks could be removed from her hard water. At the end of the ad, she called out **"Hey Culligan Man"**.

Water softeners work by removing the calcium and magnesium ions in water that can form the rocks in hard water and makes hard water bitter. These ions eventually combine with carbon dioxide to form insoluble compounds (rocks) that can plug up water heaters and destroy boilers. The process involves ion exchange where a soluble ion like sodium is exchanged for a calcium or magnesium ion.

While ion exchange burst forth after WWII, the process had been studied earlier in 1850 by Harry S. Thompson, an agriculturist and independently by John Holmes Way, a chemist, for treating soils. In 1935, Holmes and Adams produced synthetic ion exchange resins to treat industrial water supplies. Later, G. F. D'alelio produced synthetic ion exchange resins at the General Electric Company.

Like all great inventions of man, God is many times the first to the Patent Office. He was aware of the process many years before the Manhattan Project and actually used it in saving the Israelites during their trek in the desert.

When they came to Lake Marah (Ex 15:23-25) they found that the water was bitter and they couldn't drink it. The Israelites then murmured to Moses. He didn't know what to do, until God told him to throw a tree into the lake and the water became sweet.

What had happened is that the tree had lain in the sun for a long time and the cellulose became oxidized to the point where it was an ion exchange resin and absorbed the calcium and magnesium ions, making the water sweet.

So when that lady in the ad calls for the Culligan Man, she really is calling for Moses, who was the **First Culligan Man.**

DEUS SILICUM NON SUNT URANUS

In Psalms 24: 1 David sings, "The earth is the Lord's and the fullness thereof". This clearly indicates that this world we live in is certainly not ours to despoil; since we don't own it. It's like a child's sandbox, which becomes a world to him and many childlike games and dreams can be built in it.

One of the problems with outdoor sandboxes is that they must be covered to keep cats from messing in the sand during the night. As a result they are covered or the child's play area will be ruined. In a similar manner, God has his sandbox, which is our earth. He allows us to play in it, but we have not done a very good job taking care of it.

In early Biblical History, man began to disobey the rules and foul up the sand box. This first incident was Adam and Eve's fall for which we still suffer today. Next came the corruption of the races, such that God sent the Flood to destroy the wicked. Shortly after that Babylon rose and ruined His sandbox, so He confused their languages. The rise of Sodom and Gomorrah was where man sank to the lowest ebb of human behavior, such that God sent two of His angels to check on the situation (Gen 19). The men of Sodom tried to attack these angels who blinded them, then destroyed Sodom and Gomorrah.

Over the intervening years, civilizations have risen and been destroyed as they depart from God's law and destroy his sandbox. Much of these destructive forces come from within. Witness the rise and fall of Babylon, Greece, Rome, England, Russia and now the United States on the pinnacle of its rise and soon heading for the same fate as its predecessors.

We don't need to look to far to see how we are destroying God's sandbox. We decimate the forests, oceans, whales and other marine animals, pollute the air, water and soil and continue to do so urged on by our own greed and reckless abandon of God's principles. In addition to destroying the physical environment, we are destroying our spiritual environment by encouraging homosexuality, abortion, pornography, drugs and even blasphemy.

Scientists are warning us of near misses of our earth by wandering satellites and comets and the irreparable damage we are doing to our air and water. It's like a Petri dish in which microorganisms grow. As the organisms grow, they produce alcohol that accumulates until it kills the entire population in their own waste. What we need to do is to stop messing in God's sandbox or He will surely take steps to wipe us out. We should remember this:

Deus Silicum non sunt Uranus*

* Don't piss in God's sandbox

DOG STORY

The Bible is a treasure of information and actually the Owner's Manual for Mankind. If all of the teachings of Jesus were included, there could not be enough books to contain it all (Jn 20:25). As a result, only key information is included and other important facts must be added by concerned writers to expand on the wonders of God's Kingdom. Such a tale would include God's first creation that is not recorded in the Bible, but is clearly understandable from this essay.

When God pondered His first creation, He realized that such a creature must possess Love, Loyalty, Caring, Understanding and Devotion. Such a creature would respect all the beautiful creatures, trees and plants in His Kingdom. After several design sketches He came up with a creature that had these properties. His first creation walked on four legs, was black and followed Him everywhere. God was so impressed with this creature He decided to give it a name. After pondering on this, God came up with a brilliant idea.

"I'll give Him my name spelled backwards" He said.

So this is how the dog got its name.

Now Dog loved God very much. Dog looked like a Labrador retriever and went everywhere God went. When God left for work, Dog would follow Him to the gate and watch Him until he disappeared in the distance. Poor Dog was very lonely until the end of the day when He would see God coming up the path. God would be tired after a busy day creating the stars, galaxies and everything we now have. What pleased Him so much was to see Dog waiting eagerly for Him at the gate. Dog would wag his tail, bark and jump for joy. He would follow God into the house and stay with Him until bedtime. At night Dog would sleep at God's feet and also keep a careful ear for any strange sounds.

Everything was so good with God and Dog until one day God let Dog follow Him to work. Dog sniffed everything he could and ran circles around God till He got to His office. One day, Dog was lying on the front step of God's office when an Archangel went by. Dog had not seen an Archangel before so he thought it would be fun to chase him. The Archangel ran for his life then finally took flight to escape Dog. Although Dog thought this was fun, he soon found out that this was not the proper thing to do. Several other angels also complained to God about Dog. God did not want to hurt Dog, so He decided to create a companion for Dog; especially since God was getting busier with all the creation work.

So God made man in His image and likeness to keep Dog company. Dog and man got along well; even though Dog never forgot the wonderful times he had being so near his God. We say that "Dog is man's best friend" yet we should remember that the dog is also God's best friend.

And so, this is how and why the dog was created. Though man has lost sight of the Creators' need for us to care for His Kingdom, the dog still has all the wonderful traits that God had required in His final design.

So the next time you see a beautiful dog remember that the dog was the first creature created and that the wonderful traits which God planned, Love, Loyalty, Dependability and Caring are all wrapped up in that creature with the wagging tail.

$E=mc^2$

During the last half of the previous century, a number of intellectual giants emerged who laid the foundation for the technology base of the twentieth century. Men like James Clerk-Maxwell who developed the electromagnetic theory, Max Planck who developed the Quantum Theory and Albert Einstein who developed the Photoelectric Theory of conduction of electricity in gases are a few of these giants. (The photoelectric cell that protects you from a closing elevator door was the practical result of Einstein's theory.)

One of Einstein's greatest contributions was his General Theory of Relativity which was not well understood and unproven in its early stages giving rise to much skepticism. The general public recognizes this theory in its simplistic form as given in the title of this essay. What it says is that energy (E) and mass (m) are inter convertible and related to the speed of light squared, (c^2). What this says is that matter should be changeable into energy and vice versa. A remarkable example of this theory is the explosion of a nuclear bomb or the reactions that are undergone in a nuclear power plant to generate electricity. Here matter, plutonium is converted to energy. But what about the reverse direction?

This concept must work since as an electron is accelerated closer to the speed of light, its' mass increases significantly; thus confirming the theory.

I like to think of simpler examples of proof of Einstein's theory in recorded events of significance to Christians. We have several examples that followed the tragic events of Good Friday, when Jesus rose from the grave. Scripture records the immense light emanating from the tomb; possibly the conversion of Jesus' body to energy so that He could pass through the sealed tomb's enormous door. (The other plausible explanation recorded is that angels rolled the stone away that is also credible [Matt

28:2,3]). His enormous brightness also would indicate a great change from mass to energy. But, how do we explain the way Jesus suddenly disappears from his disciples at Emmaus then coming through the walls in the upper room? (Lk 24:36). Jesus, as author of all things is surely conversant with Einstein's theory, probably should be called Jesus theory as taught by Einstein, and as ruler of the universe is master of the ability to convert mass to energy at will. The numerous examples of His emerging to visit with his apostles show clearly his mastery of the inter convertibility of mass to energy. Going further, how do we explain the manner in which angels materialize to interact with people. Angels appeared to Abraham on their way to destroy Sodom and Gomorrah (Gen 18:2) and dine with him. We know that angels are spiritual creatures, how then do they materialize to interact with people other than being able to inter convert from energy to mass? Clearly, this simple equation may hold the key to the great secrets of the entire universe and more importantly, to the Glory of our God, who is Master of the Universe and all that are in it. One of the great anticipations for Christians is that someday we too shall understand $E=mc^2$ and be able to convert between matter and energy as He surely did on that great Resurrection Day when He finished the most important mission ever accomplished on this Earth!

FIG TREE

Early this spring we potted a fig tree and waited for it to bud. Unfortunately, though its stock was green, the tree failed to produce leaves. Later, Carol suggested that I plant the fig in the garden just in case it might grow; I did this and forgot about it.

One day Carol told me she had a surprise for me…the fig tree did grow and was doing very well. This was very pleasing to us and now I want to be sure it will survive the winter so I potted it and moved it into the garage till next spring.

The other evening, as I placed the tree in the garage, I thought about the fig tree and all of the references to fig trees in the bible. There is the story of our future when each man can sit under his own fig tree; Zacchaeus who ran ahead of Jesus and climbed a fig tree to see Him and was rewarded by having Jesus come to his home. (Lk 19:1-10). [Scripture mentions a sycamore; some say it was a fig tree].

Another reference to a fig tree speaks of the comparison of Israel to a fig tree which loses its fruit before maturity. Still another and very significant prophecy is that of Jesus speaking of the end times where He cautions to "look at the fig tree, and the other trees, when they begin to bud forth, summer is nigh" (Matt 24:32). Many believe that this prophecy was fulfilled in 1948, when at last, Israel returned to their homeland after 2,000 years of captivity.

One of the most dramatic encounters with the fig tree occurred at the end of Jesus' career on earth. One morning on His way to the temple, He was hungry and seeing a fig tree He rushed up to obtain some fruit, but there was none. Jesus cursed the fig tree then proceeded to the temple where He drove out the moneychangers. (One might wonder if the fig tree disappointment may not have catalyzed His wrath when He came to the temple) (Mk 11:12-26).

There are a number of things here to consider. First, Jesus surely knew that fig season was not on and should not have expected to find figs thereon. More startling however, was the next day, when they passed by and the apostles noted that the tree had shriveled up and died. Here Jesus taught them a great lesson. He pointed out that if you have enough Faith, you can move a mountain and cast it into the sea. His curse of the fig tree was clear evidence of such power.

There is also a great lesson here for us. We must be prepared at all times, for we never know just when He may come for us. The fig tree had its entire life to prepare for a visit by the King of Kings and blew it. The condemnation of the fig tree also shows the powerful wrath of God when He judges...no second chance! This means that we too must be prepared for His sudden coming, not on our terms, but on His.

Finally, while the lesson here was harsh, there is hope in Faith, where He teaches the importance of Faith and the sheer power of Faith in not only drawing near to Jesus, but in helping us to prepare for that sudden, unexpected visit by the Lord of Lords. With Faith and His undying Love, we should, unlike the fig tree, be prepared when He comes seeking us.

WHO'S YOUR FRIEND?

I couldn't help but notice you recently. I don't know you personally, but for some reason, you have caught my eye and piqued my interest in you.

I have always been interested in the tableau of people and made a hobby of watching people and their behavior. Many people telegraph their inner feelings in their demeanor. In some cases I can detect the anger in their eyes or the anxiety in their expression. Many people project their mission; going from one place to another or coming from one place, then off to another. It seems that we are all preoccupied with our missions; many of which are of little value in them, but which control our goings to and fro.

But, what interests me about you is that you seem to be at peace with yourself and your surroundings. When you enter a room, you seem to project, that is, radiate something, maybe an aura, which sets people at ease. You remind me of a priest I once knew, Father O'Brien, an author and professor at Notre Dame. One day I was returning from a trip and our plane to South Bend had been delayed. When we finally boarded the flight, you could cut the tension with a knife. People were fumbling with their overcoats, hats and luggage, impatient and actually hostile. Yet, after everyone was seated something strange happened. The last passenger to board was Father O'Brien. As he came down the aisle, he had a pleasant smile. He radiated an aura that spread a calm all through that airplane's cabin. I felt that someone special had come aboard who brought and gave freely; tranquility and calm.

But, back to you.

In watching you I notice that you see a lot. I've observed you watching a flock of geese flying overhead with a real appreciation for their presence in your life. The way you look at plants, flowers, the clouds, the sunsets and even the rain, with a sincere appreciation for the Author of these great gifts. I always feel that you seem to be traveling with someone at your side. You don't act like you are alone and that someone has a very special place in your heart.

Does that someone speak to you?

Is He real? What is He like?

I wish I knew, because your whole life seems to be wrapped up with that silent, invisible companion, who makes you something so special.

Do I know your Friend? Would He talk to me too?

I wonder.

HOW LONG?

Jimmy lived in the country away from the city. Near his home, there was a beautiful lake surrounded by a meadow, some woods and fields. Jimmy and his friend Willie loved to go down to the lake to watch all the animals, birds and fish. There were cardinals, crows, finches, robins and many other beautiful birds. Other creatures included butterflies; chipmunks, squirrels, rabbits and now and then he would see a fox.

One day as Jimmy and Willie were sitting by the lake watching all the action around them, they began to wonder how long it would take to create these creatures. For example, the butterflies are very delicate, but have beautiful colors. Wouldn't you think that it would take a long time to paint the beautiful colors on such an insect. And what about a caterpillar? With all the legs on a caterpillar, it would surely take a long time to make one of these crawly creatures.

Willie did not know the answer, but his uncle Fred always came down to the lake to fish. "Why don't we ask him", Willie said. So the two boys got on their bikes and rode down to the edge of the lake where Uncle Fred was fishing.

"Do you know how long it takes to make some of these creatures" they asked Uncle Fred.

Uncle Fred was quiet for a few minutes, then told them that these creatures are made by God in the time it takes for one of you to blink your eye. That is not much time is it? The boys were impressed!!

"But", Uncle Fred said, "There is one creature that takes a long time for God to make". "Do you know what animal that is?" asked Uncle Fred.

The boys thought about it for awhile and suggested a bird, a whale, a horse, but they were all wrong. Finally Uncle Fred told them that it was the Dog!!! It takes God eight hours to make a dog. The reason it takes so long is that God spends 7 hours and 59 minutes just to make the nose. After that God can quickly finish the job in less than a minute.

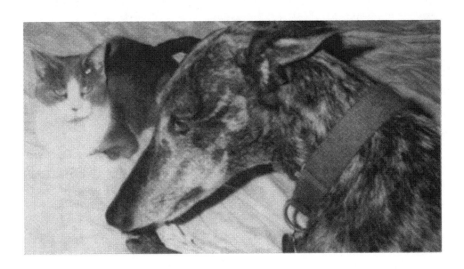

HYDROGEN FROM WATER

One of the most remarkable chemicals in the Periodic Table is hydrogen. This is the simplest of atoms and one necessary for life.

An important phase of any civilization is its reliance on energy. When energy sources are depleted the civilization can collapse.

Today we are very dependent on non-renewable energy sources, coal and oil. It would be remarkable if we could develop an energy source from a reusable resource i. e. water.

Water is composed of two atoms of hydrogen and one of oxygen. Water is also a stable inorganic compound and decomposed slowly over 1000° centigrade. Water can be decomposed into hydrogen and oxygen by electrolysis...an energy consuming process. Hydrogen can also be liberated from water in the presence of the alkali metals like sodium or lithium.

During the phony energy crisis of the seventies, efforts were directed to producing hydrogen by a number of means. One approach was to radiate titanium doped electrodes with ultraviolet light to free hydrogen.

Why do we want to obtain hydrogen for an energy source?

Well, hydrogen is an excellent fuel; light in weight and when it burns it produces no pollutants. The by-product water would be available for reuse.

What scientists need to do is to develop a catalyst that can free hydrogen from water. While this may seem impossible from thermodynamic considerations, I don't think it is impossible.

For years it was believed that polyethylene could not be formed from ethylene because of the high heat of reaction. Early organic textbooks listed ethylene as a nonpolymerizable monomer.

The British succeeded in producing polyethylene in 1933 using high pressures and temperatures. Later in 1952, Dr. Karl Ziegler in Germany discovered a catalyst that produced polyethylene at room temperature and atmospheric pressures.

This is why I believe we should have a major project to develop a catalyst to decompose water and make us energy free forever, using hydrogen as our energy source.

IMPOSSIBLE

Many years ago, a college chemistry professor told her husband that it was impossible for silicon and carbon to form compounds. Not being a chemist, her husband decided to do the impossible and devised a furnace to make silicon carbide. Thus, in 1891 carborundum became a reality as E.G. Acheson did the impossible.

If we look through history, perhaps the greatest feats of accomplishing the impossible are found in the Bible. Noah was scoffed at when he tried to build an ark (Gen. 6) and Moses did the impossible when he parted the Red Sea (Ex. 14:16) and made the bitter waters sweet (Ex. 15:25).

Other examples of impossible feats include Elias feeding the widow of Serapta for three and a half years (1 Kings 17:13-16) and Elisha raising the widow's son (II Kings 4:32-35) and curing Naaman of Leprosy (II Kings 5). Other examples of impossibles must include Daniel surviving the lion's den, his companions surviving the firey furnace and David slaying Goliath.

The New Testament provides numerous feats of impossibilities from feeding the 4,000 (Matt. 15:36-38), healing the man with the withered hand (Matt 12:13), walking on water (Matt. 14:25), healing the sick (Matt 12:36) and raising Lazarus (Jn 11:43-44).

By far the greatest impossible must be Christ's resurrection from the dead. This single feat overshadows all impossible feats in that it overcame death, sin and purchased for us eternal salvation. Here, all feats no matter how awesome, cannot compare to this great event. Fortunately for us, we are the beneficiary of this impossible feat and should bear in mind how much He cared to perform this for us -truly **a remarkable expression of His love for us.**

Luke said it best in a single line: (Lk 1:37

"For with God, nothing shall be impossible".

INTERVENTION

There are so many problems facing the world today that appear to be more and more insoluble. It would be great if we could have some kind of intervention that would resolve our many man-made problems and restore the earth to a more livable place. The best possible intervention would be to have God step in and take over, but this appears remote.

It is interesting that in this day and age, we do not have prophets like Moses and others who have a direct line to God as he and others had. On the other hand skeptics would discount divine intervention out of hand. Yet, it is interesting that when the Israelites were at the bottom of their well of despair, God intervened and appeared to Moses in the burning bush. At the height of the Roman terror in Caesar's time, God sent John the Baptist and finally the ultimate savior, Jesus himself!!

Does God intervene in people's lives today? Is this possible?

91

I am reminded of a story about a young preacher who was fresh out of Divinity school who started on an Evangelical Mission. He set up a weeklong revival in Los Angeles in a large tent and began his ministry. By Wednesday it was obvious that his mission was a failure as he looked out at all the empty chairs. He decided that they would fold their tent on Friday night. On Thursday night, a woman attended his revival and was so impressed, that she went home and phoned William Randolph Hearst. Now Mr. Hearst lived in a castle in San Simeon, north of Los Angeles, and was virtually impossible to reach by phone, since there were six intervening secretaries between him and any ringing phone. Yet, when the lady phoned, it was Hearst himself who answered.

She told him that she had heard the young preacher that night and felt that he truly had a message and should have support for his ministry. Hearst listened, hung up, and sent a wire to all his news bureaus with two simple words, **PUMP GRAHAM.**

You might imagine the shock that Friday evening when Billy Graham's tent was overflowing with news reporters, flash and movie cameras as they listened to his message, then broadcast it to the world.

Do you think that God would have intervened in this event?

There are too many impossibilities for this to be just a case of coincidence. What is more important is that God chose to use Billy Graham as a messenger for His work. When you think about how many have heard the word of God as a result of Rev. Graham's ministry you can clearly see that God, in His plan, realized that intervention here would be of great benefit to the Human Race and all those seeking the Kingdom of God.

How has God intervened in your life? If you examine your past in detail, I am certain you can find at least one example where God in His infinite mercy has intervened to help you on your way to Salvation.

KINGDOM

As children we probably encountered the term KINGDOM in the fairy tales and fables that rendered accounts of good and bad kings and of entrapped maidens whose lives were saved by a prince. Recall the touching story of the Sleeping Beauty and of Snow White and the Seven Dwarfs. Another mention of kingdom is from our school books where the Animal Kingdom is frequently referenced. One common aspect of a kingdom is that there is a singular ruler, usually a king or one whose title means king, and one who is totally in charge, and one who virtually owns everything within the kingdom. His subjects owe him subservience that is rendered by love, fear, need or by threat of bodily harm or death or combinations thereof.

Kingdoms vary from extremely small ones to those covering, in many cases, of the known world. Kingdoms usually vary in degrees of kindness extended to subjects. Many start out good, but eventually the power to rule leads to corruption, which eventually brings down a kingdom or is reflected in terrible treatment of its subjects.

Recall how King David became a powerful ruler, but eventually was overcome by the material good and lusts of worldly temptations. As a result, his subjects suffered the consequences of his demise and the kingdom eventually collapsed.

Alexander the Great ruled all the known world, but his kingdom was short lived. He died at the age of 33! Therein lies the key flaw in all earthly kingdoms - they are finite. The greatest king who ever lived was Nebuchadnezzar. This great king has never been surpassed on this earth. He was such a great king that even God told him so (Dan 2:37). In fact, when Daniel prophesied about the king's dream, Nebuchadnezzar was depicted as having a head of gold - gold representing the most precious metal and most valued object. Yet, in spite of all his greatness, he and his kingdom were finite. After his death, his kingdom was eventually divided and the glory of Babylon ceased to exist.

The Roman Empire, is one of the greatest kingdoms, also collapsed. Witness the British Empire, at one time in this century, the sun never set on the British Empire. Yet today it is reduced to a small island with a little potency.

This then, is a common characteristic of a worldly kingdom - they all have an end - they are finite. This is fortunate because in many cases, as kingdoms degrade and become more cruel or oppressive, there is satisfaction or hope that they will collapse and the subjects will have another chance. Witness the Japanese, German, Italian and now the Soviet empires. It also seems that a common trend is from Good to Bad, but never in the opposite direction.

So much for worldly kingdoms. But, there are other great kingdoms that are of the spirit world. What about these?

In the realm of the spirit world, there is a kingdom which seems to last forever. This is the kingdom ruled by Satan - the Prince of this World. But, even this kingdom is doomed - it will not last forever. Jesus spoke of this and clearly pointed out that Satan's rule was at an end. He has been convicted; Satan is now free on bond, but will be sentenced and his kingdom destroyed (John 16:11). So too, spirit kingdoms can have their downfalls.

THE KINGDOM OF GOD

There is one kingdom that is in contradiction to all of the above - and that is the Kingdom of God. This is a spiritual kingdom, but is also a promised worldly kingdom that will be established by God himself (Rev 21:10).

This great Kingdom has a central theme - that of Love, Goodness, Peace and one which has no end! Just what is the nature of such a Kingdom, what is the promise and what is it like?

THE FIRST KINGDOM

The Kingdom of God is described in Genesis Chapter 2. Here Adam and Eve lived in a kingdom free from evil - a perfect paradise. But, by the craft of Satan, this kingdom was set aside for a time when Adam and Eve fell for Satan's lies. In spite this great loss, God in His infinite mercy provides a second chance (Gen. 3:15) in alluding to a promised redeemer.

After the fall, it was all down hill. The first murder (Gen. 4:8) followed by sexual perversion (Gen. 6:2, 5, 19:5). God intervenes twice to stop the degradation, first by destroying the earth by water, then by singling out Sodom and Gomorrah (Gen. 19:28).

FOREVER

The first hint of the everlasting comes very beautifully in the discourse thats Moses had with God on the mountain of God where Moses found the burning bush (Ex 3:2). As Moses seeks identity, God replies that His name is I AM and that it is His name forever (Ex. 3:15).

When David was anointed King of Israel, the prophet Nathan predicts that he would build a Temple of the Lord and that God will establish a kingdom that will last forever (2 Kings 7:13). At this point Nathan is predicting the rise of Solomon, David's son, who was a great king, but foresaw the coming of the King of Kings, Jesus Christ, many years hence.

Moving on we find more prophesy relating to the coming of the Kingdom of God - the Everlasting Kingdom. The prophet Isaiah correctly predicts the Virgin Birth (Isa. 7:14) and the coming of a true King, one whose government rests upon His shoulders, a Kingdom of Peace and an everlasting Kingdom both spiritual and material (Isa. 9: 6,7). This promise is beautifully amplified musically in the Messiah by George F. Handel. The nature of the Kingdom is then described in detail by the prophet Isaiah to show that Justice, Peace, Mercy and Love are cornerstones of its foundation

- these are all spiritual. But, he goes on to explain the material aspect of the Kingdom in beautiful detail - the lion shall eat straw like the ox and the child will play at the den of the asp - all evil is removed - Satan and his evil kingdom are destroyed (Isa 11: 1-10).

We have further evidence of the everlasting Kingdom of God from the prophet Daniel. After interpreting King Nebuchadnezzar's dream, Daniel points out that God will establish His Kingdom and that His Kingdom is an everlasting one which will consume and destroy all the other kingdoms. The kingdoms of this world have no chance. They are not based on the Love of God and all are doomed!

Daniel makes other references to the coming of Christ and to the establishment of His everlasting Kingdom (Dan 9:24,26). The prophet Malachi describes the impressive coming of Christ not as a meek child, as He did the first time, but as a powerful ruler against whom no one can stand - a King of might and splendor (Mal 3:1,2).

So much for Old Testament references to the Kingdom of God and its everlasting nature. We should bear in mind that this promise is of profound significance. It was first made by God himself, then reaffirmed by the angels, and finally by Jesus himself.

THE COMING KINDGOM

The stage is now set - after a long wait, the promise is beginning to unfold. Perhaps the most moving descriptions are found in the Gospel of Luke. When the angel Gabriel appeared to Mary, she pointed out that her child shall be great and that His Kingdom will have no end (Lk 1:33)

Let us now examine the nature of this Kingdom. Jesus describes the Kingdom in many beautiful ways. For example, He illustrates that although He welcomes all to His Kingdom, we cannot take it for granted. He illustrates this in the Parable of the Wedding Feast where He invites people, but in their lust for the materials of this world, they refuse to attend the wedding. Eventually, He destroys the wicked that refuse and accepts all others. In spite of this, the man who came unprepared was cast out (Matt 22).

In other descriptions, Jesus compares the Kingdom of God to a man who sowed good seed and an enemy sowed weeds. Jesus points out that while both will co-exist (as we have evil and good in the world today) at the establishment of the Kingdom, the evil will be destroyed forever and the good gathered into His Kingdom (Matt 13: 24-30).

Jesus also compares the Kingdom to a grain of mustard seed which grows into a large tree, where the birds of the air come and rest in its branches (Matt 13:31-32). Have you ever seen the birds at eventide fly to their rookery at the close of a day? They come from all directions, as if He is calling them to the shelter of the trees, where they will have safety for the night. What a beautiful reminder of this parable and of the Kingdom of God. Other examples include the leaven that a woman buries in flour, until all the dough has risen. This graphic illustration is easily demonstrated in making bread - a vivid reminder of Christ's salvation - where the Love of God can be spread to all who will receive it (Matt 13:33).

Finally, the Kingdom of God is like a man who finds a pearl, then goes and sell all his pearls to buy the real thing (Matt 13:46). This parable can be compared to finding a good friend - one who stands above all others, who radiates love, kindness and all the good things God has in store. Such a friend can bring Joy, Peace, Love and one who is sought after, needed and wanted. One can soon place his every thought toward that friend in many meaningful ways.

In like manner, we must have the same desire to seek after the Kingdom of God, which has been promised, assured and is clearly coming to us soon. A Kingdom characterized by **LOVE, PEACE and the Everlasting Presence of God.**

> "Seek you first the Kingdom of God
> And all these things will be added
> unto you besides".

LAW

"Obey the Law" is an old truism which if not heeded can cause serious consequences for the lawbreaker. There are two kinds of laws: the natural or God's law and civil or man's law. While laws are designed not to be broken, laws are frequently broken and the consequences have longterm impact. Laws apply to individuals and to nations. History is paved with sad stories of broken laws and the havoc wreaked by doing so.

An example of a natural law is the law of gravity. Any object, not supported, will by law, fall toward the center of the earth. An individual can disobey this law by stepping out of a ten-story window, but the result is terminal. In a similar fashion, the civil law required that we stop at a stoplight. Disobeying this law may or may not cause an immediate problem, but the continued disregard of the law could result in a traffic ticket, an accident and in some cases the loss of life.

Adam and Eve are credited with a lot of 'firsts'—First parents, first to see God face to face, first to enjoy the fruits of His kingdom and first to break the law - God's law!

This was monumental because all the evil and troubles in the world today may be laid at the foot of this first offense-breaking the law; breaking God's law. (Gen. 3:6). With the capable assistance of Satan, Adam and Eve received assurances that there would be no penalty - but actually a reward - "You will be like God"- (Gen.3:5). Since that awesome moment, all creation has suffered even to this day.

In today's society, we throw sand in the face of our Creator by ignoring God's laws:-people living together without the benefit of marriage, abusing our bodies with drugs, alcohol and tobacco, and poisoning our minds with sewage from TV showing incest, murder, adultery, bribery, deceit and immorality. These are flaunted daily before our eyes such that it seems to be the acceptable thing to do. Shows like Knots Landing, Falcon Crest, Dallas and the Soaps and their stars are revered as some kind of gods. As a country, we are to reap the rewards of our folly as we dig our graves for our enemies to bury us. The early Romans were busy attending games while the barbarians were scaling the walls of their cities. Today we ignore the potential loss of our freedom watching sports on TV while our enemies are busy devouring our economy and our way of life. All the while we slam the door in the face of God by denying prayer in our schools.

Being perfect, God must have created a true paradise. Imagine an environment whose temperature was excellent, a good food supply and all of God's creatures living in perfect harmony. The system was complete. Consider a cow. This large beast feeds on a simple diet of grass and provides milk for its young and for man. Its waste products go to restore the ground so that a continuous food supply can be assured.

In our society little thought is given to the total system; buy fast food then throw the containers on a neighbors front lawn or on the highway. Build a manufacturing plant and throw the waste products into the air and pristine streams such that even fish cannot survive.

In paradise, the food supply must have been in perfect harmony with the needs of its occupants. Man, like animals, must have eaten nuts and fruits and grasses (wheat). We have examples of fruit and nuts that bear continuously such as the macadamia nut and the mango. It is interesting to see a mango with flower, young and mature fruit on the same tree. The macadamia nut produces continuously. God could then feed all residents of paradise with a perfect ecosystem.

The psalmist reminds us that "the earth is the Lord's and the fullness thereof" (Ps 24:1) and James tell us "every good gift and every perfect gift is from above" (Jas 1:17). So then, in the beginning all was perfect, but man stepped in and made negative corrections and ruined a paradise. During the recent space flights, it became clearly apparent that the earth is a delicate ecosystem. The astronauts gained a deeper respect for the earth and its endangered environment as they circled this tiny blue jewel in space. A good example of our potential problems can be observed by looking at a small ecosystem, a petri dish. Here under proper conditions of temperature and with a food supply, bacteria or yeasts can grow at a very rapid rate. If sugar is the food supply, it is ingested as food and waste products are discharged as a gas, carbon dioxide, and as a liquid, ethyl alcohol. This is marvelous up to a point, but as on earth, the yeast do not provide for waste disposal and eventually die as the alcohol content reaches a critical level and the yeast are destroyed in their own sewage.

This same process exists on earth, thus the concern of the astronauts and those who recognize the problem. Let's look at a critical scenario of uncontrolled waste disposal. Much of our solid wastes are deposited in landfills. General Motors, for example, ships their solid wastes miles from Detroit, but as landfills become exhausted they move further away as far as 50 miles from a plant site. This cannot go on forever! Similarly, we have been burning coal for many years in electric generating plants with no regard for sulfur dioxide emissions. When mixed with moisture, sulfur oxides form sulfurous and sulfuric acids (acid rain) and depletes forests, ruins lakes and destroys fish and water flora. In addition to acid rain, electric power plants and automobiles produce tons of carbon dioxide that is absorbed by plants and in the oceans. It has been estimated that the Amazon basin produces about 18% of the world's oxygen supply, yet man is destroying the jungles of the Amazon, and other parts of the globe, at an alarming rate of 12,000 acres per hour! Vegetation is the earth's skin. Without 10% of its skin, an animal will die. The earth is close to losing 10% of its skin now. The Sahara was once a verdant land. If you want to see what the earth could look like, take a pair of binoculars and look at the moon. A more serious consequence of carbon dioxide pollution is that this gas is an insulator and keeps the heat of the earth from radiating to outer space. If our earth warms a few more degrees, the equilibrium concentration of carbon dioxide in sea water will shift pumping tons of this gas into the atmosphere creating a hot house effect and triggering ice cap melting, drowning of coastal cities and changes in our food supply.

For over fifty years, we have discharged chlorofluorocarbons into the atmosphere with impunity as aerosols, foams and refrigerants. Scientists have proposed that these chemicals eventually reach the upper atmosphere and cause depletion of the ozone layer that screens out ultraviolet radiation. Over 500 million pounds of CFC's are produced in the U.S. annually. More dangerous are nitrosyl radicals, from auto emissions that ane more effective in depleting ozone.

We now have a petri dish analogy on a global scale, but the net result will be the same.

Can you imagine God creating such a mess? Did God prepare a disposable earth that is used and abused by man then discarded? The prophet said "One generation passes and another comes, but the earth abides forever."(Eccl 1:4) Evidently, God did not make a throwaway world. The reason we have a throwaway world is because of man's folly—breaking God's law and now paying the awesome price. Natural law provides balance. Man destroyed the wolf on Isle Royale and the moose population fell apart. Disease struck the herds and the number of healthy moose fell. When the wolf was reintroduced, a balance was restored and healthy moose herds now roam the island. One of God's most remarkable creatures is the whale, yet man in his ignorance and disregard for His law has almost driven them to extinction. Chemists can synthesize all the compounds that are obtained from the whale including sperm oil, so there is no further need to destroy these marvelous creatures. Mankind is on a runaway slide towards disaster because of disregard for God's law from the beginning. How close we are to total destruction is not easy to determine; but one thing is certain, we are headed for disaster.

Fortunately, as in a Lone Ranger serial, help is on the way. In spite of man's disregard for God's law, God has not turned his back on man. He sent His only Son to save us from ourselves and from the power of Satan. The operation is a success. Jesus defeated Satan in the desert and on Calvary. He destroyed death for all time and purchased salvation with His precious blood. If only we could wake up to the danger around us-put our moral house in order and obey God's law, we could have a paradise restored. Jesus promised us a new heaven and a new earth (Rev 21:1-4) and that He would make all things new (Rev 21:5). All the laws in the world that have ever been written or have yet to be written pale in the presence of the law given by Jesus from God: **LOVE GOD, LOVE NEIGHBOR.**

Those four words have more power than all the manmade power on earth and will be the force of law that will rule a paradise on earth when He comes again in Glory.

THE LIE

As a teacher, I like to challenge my students to try to find out who invented some of the great plastics that we have today. If one wonders about who invented nylon, or how Teflon^R was discovered, he would be led to some giant who through persistence, curiosity or serendipity made a significant discovery. With **nylon,** it was the dedicated work of duPont chemist, Dr. Wallace H. Carothers, while with **Teflon**^{R} it was another Dupont chemist, Dr. Roy Plunkett. These people paid a lot of attention to fundamentals and were rewarded with success.

One of the greatest fundamentals of human and spiritual nature is the **truth**. John describes Jesus as one begotten of the Father full of grace and **truth (Jn 1:14).** In other references we learn that the "**truth** will set you free" (Jn 8:32).

One of the greatest fears of evil men is the truth. Witness the Soviet Union over the last 70 years. The greatest effort of their leaders was to keep the truth from the Russian people and the other nations they enslaved, and by keeping them from the truth, they were able to keep these nations in bondage.

But, what of the flip side of truth? The other side of truth is of course the **LIE.**

What we need to know first, is who invented the **lie.** This is an easy question, since the inventor of the lie is that great Liar himself **SATAN!!.** The impact of the lie is almost as great as the impact of the truth. Let us consider some of the aspects of the lie and its cost to us spiritually and materially.

The first lie was manifest by the Father of all Liars, Satan, when he tricked Adam and Eve into believing that if they would eat of the fruit of the Tree of Life, it would do them no harm. This was the master lie for which the whole human race is now paying so dearly. First we lost Paradise, then took on all the human suffering and debasement which that lie caused.

Once the lie was established, it was quickly followed with other lies as Adam and Eve lied to God, Cain lied about Abel and on down to where the Master Liar met his match in the desert. Here Satan lied to Jesus telling Him that he could give Him all the kingdoms of the world if Jesus would adore him; or jump from the temple and not be killed. Later on Satan himself got into some real trouble when he lied to Beelzebub that Jesus had been destroyed on the cross, only to find Jesus show up in hell to recover the saints from Hell's grip.

Going down the centuries, Satan leads many people astray with the **LIE.** One of the fringe benefits of the lie is that it can be accompanied by power. Notice the rise to power of so many great leaders, who lie to their subjects. They achieve great success, but eventually, Satan comes calling and they fall hard.

Some of the impact of the lie in recent times include the lies of Stalin, Hitler, the British Government, who conned us into World War I and World

War II, the lies of Woodrow Wilson and Franklin D. Roosevelt who promised not to send our young men off to war, but reneged (lied) on their word with tragic results.

More recently, we have seen our own government caught in numerous lies and very high officials blatantly lying to their constituents. In our own country today, we are witnessing a President Clinton who seems incapable of telling the truth. All through his political campaign he lied to the voters, then when elected discarded his promises for expediency.

He seems to be an ordained Liar.

There is hardly a day in which we cannot find him or other high officials "lying like a rug". Christians must be alert to these people and watch lest they themselves don't get caught up in the big lie. One must be concerned that surely, Satan must play a significant role in the lives of these people, while using as his most important tool...**LIE.**

LIGHT

The other night we had a violent thunderstorm and shortly after the first lightning bolts struck the power went off. As it grew dark it soon become obvious how important electricity and more important, light is to our lives. As I sat there in the dark waiting for the light to return it caused me to reflect upon the importance of light in our material and spiritual lives.

The origin of light is cited in Genesis (1:14-18) in a very simplistic way and indicates how God separated light from dark. Without light, nothing prospers. Place a plant in the dark and it soon withers since light is essential for its life process. In ancient times man was a slave to the natural light source. When evening came it was time to fold up and to await the dawn. This did however provide an opportunity to delve into the spiritual aspect of light as Abraham did counting the stars by night. (Gen 15:5) As fire was discovered man was able to light his way at night. With the advent of the electric light, we were able to control darkness almost at will.

The green plant and much of life on earth depends upon light. Light provides food, shelter, warmth, serves in communication, travel and many phases of our lives. Without light much of the life style we know would vanish. There is also a spiritual light we have which provides us guidance for our moral path. The source of that light is Christ. He clearly indicated that He is the `Light of the World' (Jn 9:5).

Returning to the power shortage, I began to anticipate just when the light would return. As the hours passed, I began to miss the light more and my anticipation grew as minutes turned to hours. I knew that soon the light would return and everything would be all right again. In a similar manner, we wait in eager anticipation for the Light of the World to return to restore our spiritual light and wipe out the darkness that was cast on us from Eden.

Just as the lights came on so suddenly, surely His return will also be as sudden, but with so much more drama and glory. Let's hope that the spiritual power shortage ends soon.

LOWER YOUR BUCKETS

I read a story once about a group of survivors of a shipwreck who drifted aimlessly in a lifeboat. As days wore on, they had exhausted their drinking water and soon faced a new peril—dying of thirst. This went on for some time, until one day, they spotted a sailing ship in the distance. They were overjoyed at their imminent rescue. As the ship pulled alongside their lifeboat, they began to shout at their saviors to give them water. The Captain of the vessel in turn shouted, "**Lower your buckets!!**."

What these survivors didn't know was that they had been drifting in a part of the Atlantic Ocean near the mouth of the mighty Amazon River and were in fresh water all along. Here they had an answer to their thirst, but didn't even taste the water or bother to familiarize themselves with the conditions of the ocean in which they were traveling.

The other night, I heard a TV program in which they were asking opinions of some very notable people to determine just what the Human Race was going to do to solve the many problems extant in the world today. Most of the responses revolved around finding some superior intelligence to lead us to a better life; a lifestyle in which we could live in peace and other such comments. One respondent stated that we probably would not find one of superior intelligence until the year 3000, if we were lucky.

I thought this was interesting, since so many intellectuals are constantly searching for answers, trying to find the meaning of life and looking for intelligent life outside our solar system. Carl Sagan continues to propose programs to seek out intelligent beings in the universe and looking for the secrets of how life evolved on earth.

All of these reminds me of the crew in that ill fated life boat who were looking for water, dying in the process, while abundant water was all around them. This is exactly what is happening in our world today. We are adrift on Satan's ocean teeming with filth, depravity, hunger, suffering and with no apparent route to safety. Yet, God has provided a safe area where He has set us in a sea filled with His Love, Hope and Promise of Salvation. People are looking everywhere for a solution, when one is close at hand in the Bible. All of the answers to these complex problems can be found there in simple terms and in powerful interpretations of things past and things and events in the future. Jesus promised He would return to bring peace to the world. We have not done our part to help speed His return. God has given us all the spiritual water we need to survive. What we need to do is: LOWER OUR BUCKETS

MEETINGS

Have you ever given any thought to meetings? That's right meetings. In the business world, meetings are a perennial activity. It seems that it is one of management's key tools for accomplishing a task. Meetings have a lot of different characteristics such as length, number of attendees, location and agenda and can be as large as thousands or as small as a two person meeting. In addition, meetings can be as useless as many are or have such an impact as to change the course of an individual's life, the course of a nation or the history of the world.

Consider the meeting of a cave man with a saber tooth tiger. This could be a significant meeting with fatal results for the cave man. On the other hand, an individual struggling across the desert would welcome a meeting by his rescuers.

Let's take a look at some significant meetings and their impact and also look into the future at the most important meeting in our lives. One of the most significant meetings of all time must have been that first meeting between God and Adam when God gave him dominion over His kingdom. Imagine the awe and thrill of that great meeting. On the other hand, imagine that last meeting with God when Adam and Eve were told that they could no longer live in paradise and would be forced out. The impact of that meeting is still with us today.

Other significant meetings include the meeting of Moses and God when Moses went to inquire about the burning bush that was not consumed by the flames. At this one on one meeting, God set the course of the Israeli nation for all time.

Moving down the ages we come to other important meetings Jacob met Joseph after living for so many years thinking that his beloved son had been lost years before. The meeting of Mary and Elizabeth provides us with a good insight into the power of prophecy and its fulfillment. Later in life, the meeting of the ten lepers with Jesus illustrated the power that Jesus could command with just a simple order.

During the awesome crucifixion of Jesus on the way to Calvary, Veronica met Jesus and wiped His face, then He meets His Mother which had to be the biggest low in her life while He was on His way to purchase salvation for us with His own life.

After His resurrection, there were some remarkable meetings; the first being His meeting with Mary Magdalene; then the apostles at Emmaus; then at Jerusalem. Now nearly two thousand years since His leaving, we witness the same importance of meetings. Today the airwaves are full of stories of the many meetings going on between warring factions, large business enterprises gobbling up each other, and efforts to bring some semblance of peace or harmony on this earth.

We have recently seen large mass meetings heralding the downfall of Communism, the rallies over pollution, disease and political rallies. In our congress we see incompetent men struggling to balance the budget while keeping a good eye on saving their political necks. Fortunately, we don't have to attend these meetings and have a fairly broad choice in participating in these meetings and can avoid them quite easily.

Unfortunately, there is one face to face meeting that we are all scheduled to attend in which we have no choice but to attend and one that we cannot avoid. That meeting is the most important meeting of our lives and one to which we should all eagerly look toward. That meeting is the one where we meet our Creator, our Savior and our Lord. What a great meeting that will be; one for which we must do our best to be adequately prepared. This meeting will indeed be the final and most important meeting of our lives. Thanks to Jesus and His gift of Eternal salvation, we can look forward to that time with hope and not despair.

POWER

Power is an interesting word. The physicist defines power as the rate of doing work or the amount of work done in a unit of time. The politician defines power as the ability to get reelected, appointed to important posts or running for president. A corporate CEO would define power as the ability to control his officers and set the direction for his company. In the automotive industry we think of power in terms of horsepower, a unit defined as 746 watts of energy and is a unit used to try to overcome the competition by showing that one vehicle has more horse power that another. In a more humorous way, note the horsepower race in lawn tractors, where someone who has an 8 h.p. tractor envies his neighbor who recently purchased a 12 h.p. tractor, which cannot complete a single turn because his lawn is too small.

Power is also manifested in other ways. In people relationships power is exercised over individuals or groups such that a single command can be used to carry out a chain of events. Harry Truman's single command to use the atomic bomb against Japan created a whole new age for humanity.

Parents also exercise power over children by possessing authority and hence power to train, coerce, guide and lead their children in growing up properly. There is also an abuse of power where small people use the power of position to abuse, intimidate, cajole or threaten people to do their will.

Other forms of power are related to spiritual activities. For example, Satan and his crew have tremendous power over spirits and peoples lives using a power given to them at the beginning of the ages. This power is very strong and nearly invincible. Witness today the rise in Satanism and cults influencing the lives of many people.

Jesus also had power during his short stay on earth and exercised it on numerous occasions. Illustrations of His power include the encounter with the Centurion. The Centurion clearly recognized Jesus' power and would not allow Him to come under his roof, knowing that Jesus had the **power** to cure his servant. Jesus also uses His power to overcome temptation in the desert, where He had His first showdown with Satan and won. Jesus also knew how to use His power and had great restraint not to exercise that power, when the hypocrites condemning Him to death.

The opposite of power is powerless. There are many things in life over which we have power. But, have you ever heard someone saying that they were powerless to do something?

In so much of our lives we are powerless to do things. We cannot prevent certain accidents, illness or death. It is also difficult to have power to solve many problems in life, yet some people do seem to have the power to do extraordinary feats. Where do they find such power? Can we obtain that power to assist us in our journey through life?

I am convinced that God provides some unusual power to His people to make our way through life. Moreover, this power is really obtainable if we would only seek it and use it wisely.

How many problems have you solved which seem to be insolvable?

I recall an incident in Graduate School where my entire research program came to an abrupt halt. I could not repeat some critical experiments that I had done previously. I tried everything but with no success. Without these experiments, I could not graduate. I would load a bomb with reactants, set it up to run overnight and check it in the morning for the results. Each day produced another negative result. One afternoon I loaded a bomb with reactants, set it up and left for home. I usually walked to the Post Office, then the Grotto, then home. As I passed the Business School a loud voice shouted "**double the aluminum**".

I stopped and said, "What?

The voice repeated, "**double the aluminum**".

I replied. "o.k.", then continued on my way.

The next morning I opened the bomb and found nothing…another negative experiment. I then doubled the aluminum concentration and the next day found the bomb filled with polyethylene! I was then able to complete the rest of my experiments and graduate. I am convinced that the power of God certainly played a role in my breaking through the impassible block in my research.

I would imagine you may cite similar events. But more importantly, there is a tremendous **power** available to us and free for the asking. We should conduct our lives so that power can be available to us when we need it. If we are not at peace with our God we shall find some difficulty in acquiring that power. It is like turning a light on. The power is there, but if you do not flip the switch, there will be no light. Similarly, if we are not spiritually connected to our God, we cannot benefit from the **power** of the **Light of the World.**

RAIN, RAIN GO AWAY

Are you aware of one of the greatest miracles of our time? This happened in Portugal in 1917. Three shepherd children were tending their sheep in Fatima, Portugal one clear and beautiful day. As the children herded the sheep toward home, they heard the loud claps of thunder and lightning, even though there were no clouds in the sky at that time.

The children were frightened and ran for cover. No matter where they went, the lightning seemed to follow them. When they finally looked up into the sky, they saw a very beautiful Lady in the air looking down at them. She spoke to the children and told them that she would appear to them again.

This caused a lot of talk in the small village where they lived. The priest wanted to know whom the Lady was so they eventually were told that she was the Mother of God.

People began to gather in this small village to see what would happen when she would appear again. Eventually, the Blessed Mother told them that something big would happen on the thirteenth day of April.

As a result, thousand of people gathered to see what was going to happen. As luck would happen, this was a very cloudy and rainy day. The rain poured down and thousands of people were soaking wet as they stood in the countryside waiting for something to happen.

Then, the Blessed Virgin appeared to the children and told them to look at the sky. The sun began to spin wildly and then plunged to earth. People were frightened and thought the end of the world was at hand. The sun did this a number of times, then returning to its place in the heavens.

Suddenly, the clouds cleared and the sun shone brightly. But, what was a real surprise was that all the ground was dry, the people who were soaking wet were all dry as if nothing had ever happened.

What a great story.

ROCK

The word rock has many meanings and connotations. To the geologist, it is his tool shed, to the musician, it is a new brand of music, to the sea captain, it is something from which to steer clear and to the insurance business, it is something to compare the company soundness and provide a sense of security.

Christians consider the rock in many terms. The hymn "Rock of Ages" tells of the strength of our God in terms of a rock, while Martin Luther penned the hymn "A Mighty Fortress is our God" to reflect upon the strength and power of God.

In the Bible, there are a number of significant references where a rock plays a key role for the rock may be the key to the ending of the ages. We are familiar with Moses, who struck a rock and obtained water (Ex 17:6). Another significant event related to a rock was the success of David in slaying Goliath (1 Sam 17:49) with a single rock. This single action destroyed the Philistine army and gave Israel the opportunity to overcome their strong adversary. Jesus referred to Peter as a Rock and promised him the Keys of the Kingdom when Peter revealed to the apostles who He was (Matt 16:18). Finally, in the Last Days, men will pray that the rocks will fall on them in order to escape the wrath of God (Rev 6:16).

One of the most awesome events in the Bible is recorded in the second chapter of Daniel. Here Daniel unravels the Kings dream and describes the huge statue with a head of gold, chest of silver, legs of iron and feet of clay and iron. This huge statue is destroyed by a rock coming out of space and striking the feet of the statue. After that destruction, the Lord rebuilds a new world order.

The statue represented the greatest kingdom on earth, that of Nebuchadnezzar. The head of gold represented his kingdom and the rest of the statue the kingdoms that would succeed him. What is of most interest, is that the way in which the earthly kingdoms are destroyed, by a rock.

We have a similar situation occurring today. Just prior to and following the Persian Gulf War, President Bush called for a New World Order. The Bilderberg Group consisting of leaders from around the world and including such luminaries as David Rockefeller, Henry Kissinger, George Bush, Queen Beatrix of the Netherlands are busily planning to develop a one world government. This government will have one currency, one leader, probably the head of the United Nations, and will seek to dominate the weaker nations for the benefit of the elite ruling party. They recently met (June 6, 1991) near Baden, Germany to develop their plans.

Some of their plans include the United States financing the rebuilding of the Soviet Union to the tune of $500 billion; (Henry Kissinger publicly decries this aid, but secretly supports it), forming a Trade Free union with Mexico and Canada, Most Favored Nation status for China and continued support of Israel's mischief in the world. Eventually, the U.S. will surrender its sovereignty to the UN, such as we did in the Gulf War. The Bilderbergers will be successful and will eventually develop a One World government at the expense of the American taxpayers and at a cost of our freedom.

What will stop this?

The simplest way to stop this is with a rock; just as God did with Goliath and as suggested in Daniel. There are currently a number of asteroids circling the earth that will be the instrument of the destruction of world power. Recently, one of these rocks missed the earth by six hours. Another entered our atmosphere in a blaze of light then escaped back into space. Was this a warning? Clearly, as man continues to ravish the earth with complete disregard for fundamental teachings of God we must prepare for an end. What better way to bring this about than that already described in Daniel. Was this God's way to warn us of our own end?

SALLY'S GIFT

Sally was wondering what kind of gift she could give her mother on Mother's Day. She knew that she could ask her father for some money and they could go to the store and buy a present...but what kind of present. Mother's day was still a few weeks off and she had time to think about a gift.

One afternoon at her school, the teacher handed out a packet of wild flower seeds to the children. Sally took hers packet home and put it in a drawer and forgot about it.

One day Sally got a great idea. "I think I know what I will give my Mother on Mother's Day" she said to herself. I'll give her something from the heart and something beautiful.

Behind Sally's home was a large field where Sally and her friends would play. So Sally went out there and began digging a small circular garden in that field. After she got the dirt turned, she planted her packet of seeds and every day she would go out there with a watering can and water her garden. Her mother saw her carrying the water out to the field, but did not think much about it.

After a week of watering, Sally still had no garden. She was sad and decided that it was not the thing to do. After a few days, Sally went into the field again and much to her surprise saw some small shoots coming out of the ground. Soon there was a carpet of green as the wild flower plants began to grow. Just before Mother's day, Sally went out again and found the garden alive with all kinds of beautiful flowers.

She quickly made a Mother's Day card and laid it on the kitchen table so her Mother would see it the next day. After reading the card, Sally took her mother by the hand and led her to the field to show her mother the present. Her mother was overjoyed. She told Sally that this was truly a love gift from the heart and it made her Mother so happy…and so was Sally.

SECOND CHANCE

A few years ago, I read a most interesting book by Dr. Raymond A. Moody, Jr. entitled **"Life After Life"**. This book describes in graphic detail numerous **Near Death Experiences (NDE)** of many of his patients. He became so intrigued by this that he began a deliberate study of this phenomenon. He later wrote another book in which he coined the term NDE to describe what happens to people who become clinically dead, then are revived.

The basic tale told by most NDE people is quite similar in its basics with a few variations. In sum, it involves leaving the body, seeing the surroundings where the death occurs, then going into a dark tunnel, then finding a source of light to which they migrate. As they reach the light some are accompanied by a **'Being of Light'** who radiates love and knowledge, there is a review of one's life in great detail, and then the person is told that they must return, since their time is not yet. People who experience NDE are generally changed spiritually and have no fear of death and in many cases regret having come back to life.

A very good friend of mine died on the operating table during surgery and experienced a NDE. She later wrote me to describe the events that took place. Her parting comment was that we never need to fear death and how beautiful it is on the other side.

In looking over the literature of books published on this subject, I am amazed how much has been written. Many skeptics attribute this experience to nitrogen narcosis, carbon dioxide changes in the body and tricks that the brain plays to minimize the death process. Yet, there is so much to this that it is interesting that the scientific community has not given this more attention.

The other day as I was thinking about this, I began to wonder why people are given this glimpse of the other side and what it could possibly mean. In some writings, it is shown that there is an abundance of love and knowledge, peace and beauty there. There are also indications that humans experience life on earth as really death compared to that on the other side.

Euripides, an ancient sage, sums it up very well:

> **"Who knoweth, if to die**
> **Be but to live;**
> **And that called life by**
> **mortals, be but death"**

It seems that a soul is required to go through life on earth to appreciate what is available in the after life.

This is not too far fetched. Consider Adam and Eve who had a paradise on earth, but had no knowledge of sin. Had they not fallen to the wiles of Satan, they might still be in the Garden of Eden. But, after the fall, they had to experience death, sin, illness, inhumanity and a host of plagues which are visited to life on earth.

Perhaps by making souls serve a life sentence on earth, the Creator has provided us a meaningful and unforgettable experience of what disobedience to God can mean for eternity. What better way to assure an eternity of peace and love when a soul is now experienced in the alternative choice. And, what a marvelous solution that God set it up this way, so that by following His way, we may enjoy an eternal Kingdom free of pain, hate and sin and live forever in an overwhelming state of peace, knowledge and above all—**LOVE**.

SECRET

In the eighteen seventies, the Studebaker brothers built wagons in South Bend. It took 28 days to complete a wagon, since the paint used required a long time to dry and many coats were used, before a wagon could be sold. Patrick O'Brien invented a varnish that would cure so fast, that a Conestoga wagon could be built in a matter of days. It was so fast, in fact, that O'Brien started the Electric Priming Company. Electric then was a magic term like atomic is today. His secret formula was closely guarded, lest a competitor could learn it and offer competition. If you ever watched a spy thriller or old time movie serials, there was always a plot involving some secret formula. For example, in some cases some crazed professor develops a secret formula for preserving life, or for destroying the world. In early American history, Ponce de Leon spent much of his time looking for the magic fountain that provided eternal life.

Other examples of secret formulas include the formulae for Coca Cola, atom bomb secrets, drugs, aircraft, organization plans, patents and certain catalysts and additives which can make or break an operation. Much of the technology involved in current fuels for operating our economy are based on highly secret formulas for catalysts, which can rearrange petroleum molecules, to form products of a desired nature from otherwise useless material.

Man's curiosity is easily aroused knowing that there may be some secret formula out there and will do most anything to discover the secret, even to the point of selling his soul to obtain the secret.

Adam and Eve was tricked by Satan into believing that he possessed a secret formula (Gen. 3:4,5), but she was fooled and today we are still paying the awesome price of that deception. One of the results of that deception is the total chaos rampant in all parts of the world today. The drug scene, Middle East, our inner cities, the total disregard for life and the environment are some of the symptoms of today's troubles.

We have politicians, statesmen and religious leaders searching for solutions and looking for the secret formula with which to restore order to a crumbling situation. If only we had some plan or formula to correct these problems, this earth would be much improved. There are some formulae in hand such as the Camp David Accord, and various United Nations plans to solve problems, but none work. These are cumbersome, wordy, intangible formulae that will never work.

Is there a formula that could restore us to a paradise on earth?

The answer is yes. But, if that formula were known, would we use it to solve our problems. Answer - NO!!.

The secret formula was given some two thousand years ago and consists of four words. All of the world's problems could be solved by applying this formula across the board. The problem is that mankind will refuse to pick up the clue and use it. The tragedy of it all is that the secret formula is right before our very eyes, and we are like people on a sinking ship, who refuse to get into the lifeboat, because they cannot recognize its purpose.

That secret formula is: **LOVE GOD, LOVE NEIGHBOR**

LOST SHEEP
(To Julie)

This is a story of a young shepherd boy who lived many years ago. His name was Joel. Although he was only ten years old, he would go out with his father and older brother to tend their sheep. Joel loved to tend the sheep and to be out with them in the fields. During springtime he was especially fond of the wild flowers that grew. The sheep also liked spring because of the greener grass and the cool water that flowed from the mountain streams.

One day Joel's father called him to his side and told him that he had a surprise for him. Eagerly, he searched his father's eyes to see what the surprise would be. His father led him over behind a large rock. To Joel's surprise, he saw a tiny lamb with its mother. His father said to him, "Joel, since you love our sheep so much, I am going to give him to you". Joel was excited! He ran to the little lamb and took it into his arms. He cuddled the little wooly lamb in his arms and hugged it. His father warned him that he must take good care of the lamb and watch it at all times.

The little lamb had so much fur that Joel named him Wooley. Little Joel spent a lot of time playing with Wooley. He would run through the grass and hide, but the little lamb would always find him. Another time, he would hide behind a large rock and little Wooley would sneak up behind him and chew on his coat, much to Joel's surprise.

In the evening, Joel would tell his mother about all the things he and Wooley would do. Sometimes, his stories would sound as if he made them up, but his mother would laugh anyway and pretend they were real.

Everything seemed to be going so well for Joel and Wooley. But, Wooley was growing so fast that little Joel could hardly pick him up anymore. Wooley also would wander away from the flock looking for grass. Several times now Joel found him wandering up a high mountain. Joel would follow him and gently lead him back to the camp.

But one day while Joel was helping his father, he forgot about Wooley and the way he would go up the mountain. After working with the sheep all morning, they sat down to lunch. But, while Joel was eating and telling his father and brothers about what he and his lamb did, he suddenly noticed that Wooley was gone! Joel's little heart began to pound as he ran about looking for his beloved lamb. Finally, he decided that he must have gone up the mountain.

Joel took his little walking stick and some water in a goatskin bag and began the long climb up the mountain. Poor little Joel fell a number of times. It seemed that he would never find his good friend. After a long time, he reached the top of the mountain. He was now sobbing because he could not find his beloved lamb. Poor Joel finally threw himself on the ground and began to cry. Just then, he felt something pulling on his coat. He lifted up his head and through his tear filled eyes, he saw Wooley!

"Wooley", he cried, "where have you been?" He threw his arms around the lamb and hugged him for a long time. The little lamb was so happy he licked Joel's face.

"We must start for home now Wooley",Joel said, as he gave the lamb some water from his goat skin bag. But, just as he turned to start down the mountain, he saw four men climbing the mountain toward them. Joel was frightened. He had heard of robbers who lived in the mountains and now he was really scared.

"Why, oh why did Wooley have to run away and cause this trouble?" He said aloud.

Joel looked around and found two large rocks. He quickly led his lamb behind the rocks and told him to be quiet. The lamb sensed the danger and did as his little master ordered. Joel thought to himself that if he could hide until these robbers left, then he and Wooley could sneak back down the mountain to safety.

Joel put his arms around Wooley and held him very tightly. There was a tiny crack between the rocks which gave Joel a good view of the mountaintop and of the robbers coming up the trail. Joel's little heart pounded as the four men came closer. He wondered why they had climbed the mountain.

Finally, Joel held his breath. He whispered to be quiet just as the four men passed in front of the rock where they were hiding. Instead of going on, the men stopped there. Joel was frightened!

Would they find him and Wooley?

What did they want here?

Three of the men sat down and began talking to each other, while the other man stood looking up to the sky. Just then, something strange happened! The man who was looking up to heaven began to grow brighter. His light gray robe became as white as snow. His face became so bright, that Joel could not stand to look at his face. His three companions hid their faces under their cloaks. Joel too, pulled away from the crack in the rock and held his lamb more tightly.

Suddenly, he heard voices and he gathered up his courage to take another peek at what was going on. To his surprise, he now saw two very

113

old men with long beards talking to the man whose clothes were as white as snow.

Joel thought about all the wild stories he told his family about his adventures with Wooley, but this was beyond his wildest dreams. He couldn't believe his eyes. Just then he saw a cloud coming and it covered the mountaintop. He heard a sound like thunder in the cloud. Joel hid his face. His little lamb was so still that Joel thought he was dead.

After a while, Joel looked again and saw that the two old men were gone and the other men were lying on the ground. The man who was standing, appeared as he did before. Surely, he is no robber. Joel looked at his face and saw that he was a very kind, pleasant man. A sudden peace came over Joel; his little heart stopped pounding. Even little Wooley seemed to relax.

Joel watched as the man called to his companions to get up. As they came past the rock where Joel and Wooley were hiding, he heard the man say, "tell the vision to no one, until…"

Joel watched for a long time as they disappeared down the mountain. He then began to descend the mountain with his little friend. Joel wondered what that was. Surely, he could never tell anyone what he saw, for no one would believe him. But, he would never forget the gentle man who brought peace to him.

I wonder who He was?

SIMPLE

Have you ever looked at some of the large trees in your yard or in Grandma's woods. Can you imagine how such a tree could have been made and what makes up a tree? Would you believe that a tree is made from two simple gases…water and carbon dioxide?

One of the most amazing things about God's Kingdom is how grand it is and how some of the most wonderful things in the Kingdom are so simple. For example, Jesus taught us how to behave as human beings so we could live good lives with only four simple words…"Love God, Love Neighbor". If we could follow these simple words, there would be no major problems in our lives. This simplicity also occurs in chemistry that is the basis of all life.

Water is one of the simplest molecules. Water is made up of two hydrogen atoms and one oxygen atom. Carbon dioxide is also a simple molecule and like water is made up of only two elements, carbon and oxygen. The chemical structure of these molecules are shown here:

H-O
 \
 H

WATER

O=C=O

CARBON DIOXIDE

Notice that the water molecule is bent, while the carbon dioxide molecule is not bent. There is a good reason for this. If water were not bent like carbon dioxide then when ice freezes, it would not float.

These two chemicals are the building blocks for making sugar and a chemical called formaldehyde. Water and carbon dioxide in the presence of sunlight combine to form formaldehyde, which is also a simple gas. From this simple beginning more complex chemicals are formed which eventually make up cellulose, a sugar, which forms the structure of the tree. So you see, that even a complex object like a tree has a humble beginning and is made from two simple gases, water and carbon dioxide.

TALL TALE

The Bible continues to be the all time best seller in the world. It is not surprising that this is so, considering that the Creator is the author of its fundamentals, even though He used ghost writers like Moses, David, Luke, Paul and others. In spite of its constant popularity the Bible still has many detractors. These include those who deny the whole creation story, the divinity of Christ and the promises made to Abraham and his descendants. In addition, the miracles cited in the Old and New Testaments tend to confound the skeptics.

I am impressed by the many miracles in that some are based on simple chemistry while others require a faith to believe in the power of God. A good example of the former is the miracle that occurred at Lake Marah (Ex 15:25) where God commanded Moses to cast a tree into the waters to make the waters sweet. What really happened is that the log had laid in the sun and the cellulose was oxidized to form an ion exchange resin which, sequestered the magnesium and calcium ions making the bitter water sweet. (Moses was the first Culligan man).

While this has a logical explanation, it was God who set Moses up to carry out this miracle. Other miracles are more difficult to explain; raising Lazarus, the widow's son and feeding the 5,000 must be taken on faith. Other troubles for Bible detractors are the numerous prophecies that defy reason, yet in due time become reality. A number of examples will suffice. Isaiah predicted that a virgin would conceive and bear a child (Isa 7:14). This is an obvious contradiction to human nature, but nevertheless did occur as predicted. Micah (5:2) predicted that Jesus would be born in Bethlehem and though Mary and Joseph were from Nazareth, He was indeed born in Bethlehem. So, regardless how impossible a prophecy may appear, it does surely come to pass as written.

An interesting and somewhat troublesome prophecy is that due to Zecharias (Zech 14: 4) in which the prophet writes that His feet will stand on the Mount of Olives and the mountains will be divided from the East to the West. Such an image would require that Jesus would be a few thousand feet tall! Surely, the prophet is mistaken. However, considering all the other impossibles in the Bible perhaps the prophet is correct. Our view of God and Christ are limited by our own narrow dimensions, yet God can hold the universe in His hand. In a recently published book "A Book of Angels" by Sophey Burnham, she describes an event that might make the above more plausible. Three Soviet astronauts had been in their space station for a long time, when they suddenly saw a bright orange light outside their spacecraft. On looking, they saw seven giant figures, with wings and halos. They appeared to be several hundred feet tall and their wings were as large as those on a jetliner. The band of angels followed the spacecraft for about ten minutes then vanished.

Twelve days later the seven angels reappeared and were seen by three more scientists who reported that they were "smiling as though they shared a glorious secret". The Soviets quashed the report, but word leaked out about this encounter in 1985. This could well explain the feasibility of Zechariah's prophecy. Considering the prophecies of Zechariah and the current turmoil in the Middle East and the world situation, we must soon realize that no man can put the world back in order but Christ Himself. Surely, in the Lord's Prayer, we say "Thy Kingdom Come" and we certainly must pray that it is soon and that we may see this prophecy fulfilled in our time.

THE STAIRCASE

Many years ago in New Mexico, an order of nuns built a mission church. It was a beautiful church and they were so pleased when it was completed. As the sisters contacted the bishop to come to consecrate the new church, they discovered a major problem.

There was no stairway to the choir loft. In fact, there was no good way to install a stairway without ruining the church.

The good sisters did not know what to do. That evening as they were talking about their problem, one of the sisters suggested that they pray to St. Joseph. The other sisters agreed and they all joined in to pray to St. Joseph to solve their problem.

As you know, St. Joseph was himself a carpenter and if anyone knew how to fix a problem involving a staircase, he would surely know how.

Not many days after this a man showed up at the church with his donkey and announced to the sisters that he was there to fix the choir loft. The sisters let him into the church and went about their duties. Every day this man and his donkey showed up and he continued his work on a staircase.

One day the man and his donkey failed to show up. The sisters went into the church and found that he had built a spiral staircase without a central support and completely out of wood. It was a magnificent staircase and led upwards to the choir loft. The sister's problem had been solved.

The sisters wanted to thank this man but he was nowhere to be found. The local lumberyard had no record of him ordering lumber and he had disappeared as mysteriously as he had arrived. The staircase still stands today.

Could this have been St. Joseph?

WHAT DO YOU WANT?

Whenever we buy a product, it is usually accompanied by an owner's manual. The information contained in the manual is useful in providing operating instructions, service information, maintenance intervals and warranty information. This is true for an iron, stereo, lawnmower or an automobile. Without this manual, it is sometimes very difficult to operate or repair an appliance. Similarly, humans also have an owner's manual that provides all the information required for the proper operation, maintenance and care of our spiritual and physical well being. Without this manual, it is difficult for Christians to operate at their optimum levels. This manual of course, is the Bible!

The Bible provides a wealth of information on numerous topics. For example, in the Old Testament, the Israelites were given laws governing food (Lev. 11), health (Lev. 12,13), marriage (Lev.18), behavior (Ex 20) and management (Ex 18: 13-27). Using these laws, the Israelite nation has been able to survive down the generations, whereas it is estimated that a people can be destroyed within a period of two hundred years by intermarriage, genocide, starvation or other disasters.

The New Testament provides numerous examples of salvation and how we may acquire it. The free gift from the cross assures our spiritual survival, but the big problem is getting there amid all of the physical and mental blocks that impede our progress to salvation.

Jesus clearly recognized the spiritual needs and more importantly the physical needs of people on their way to their ultimate salvation. In fact, His first miracle involved a material need in response to His mother's request for assistance when the wine ran out. (Jn 2:1-11) Other examples can be found in the scriptures. Within both the Old and New Testament, there are numerous citations regarding help. In Matt 7:7 Jesus simply says: Ask and you will receive, seek and you shall find and knock and it shall be opened unto you. In other references it is pointed out that Jesus knows what you want before you ask so therefore, we should boldly come before the throne of Grace to seek help in time of need (Heb. 4:16)

If Jesus knows what we want before we ask, why then should we take time to ask? Somehow, we need to bring the details of our needs to Him to obtain His grace and help in solving our problems. Perhaps a good illustration of the need to detail our needs is the case of the blind man at Jericho (LK 18:35-43). When he heard that Jesus of Nazareth was passing by, He cried out with a loud voice only to be reproved by the bystanders. Nevertheless, the blind man persisted until Jesus called for him. When the blind man approached Jesus what happened? Jesus asked him what he wanted. It was quite obvious what he wanted, surely not the directions to the nearest shopping center, however Jesus made him ask for a specific need.

We also must be like the blind man and ask for what we need, even though He already knows what we want. It is also interesting to note that the blind man had the faith necessary to achieve the miracle of eyesight.

So, when you need something, ask and you will receive, but be sure to tell Him what you want. I know He would like to hear from you. (Jer 33:3)

WHO SHALL STAND?

In the third chapter of Malachi, the Prophet predicts that a messenger shall come and that the Lord shall suddenly come to His temple. Then the Prophet goes on to ask, "Who shall abide the day of His coming and Who Shall Stand when He appears? What is Malachi talking about?

We know from Daniel (Chapter 2) that there will never be a great empire ruling the world in our time. The last attempt to do this will be the European Economic Community that cannot succeed due to conflicts of Nationalism and Monetary matters. It will be like a cartel and all cartels have within them the seeds of self-destruction.

There is now a resurgence of effort to bring about a One World government by the Bilderbergers and their supporters. These schemers have been trying to organize a One World government since the fall of the European and Asian monarchies at the close of the last century. These futile attempts resulted in the League of Nations, the Soviet empire and now the United Nations. The basic goal is to subvert the people of the world and its resources under the control of an elite few. People like Kissinger, Rockefeller, Bush, and others are the pawns in the effort to bring One World Government (slavery) to the world.

The effects of these efforts can be seen by the draining of the U. S. Treasury by the Federal Reserve Bank, (not a government agency, but a private bank controlled by the Bilderbergers), surrendering our national sovereignty to the United Nations and involving us in winless wars and wasteful spending practices.

The new world leaders have an agenda which is directed to enslavement, poverty, atheistic culture and no respect for human life. This is in sharp contrast to the principles expounded by the Prince of Peace in His Sermon on the Mount.

In "The New World Order", Pat Robertson indicates that we are in the End Times and cites much evidence to illustrate his point. This should be required reading for Christians. But what is interesting is that as the planners for the New World Order move swiftly toward implementation, they would do well to find a bible and do some reading. The readings mentioned at the start of this essay would strike some real fear in their hearts.

Can you imagine these One Worlders challenging the newly arrived Lord? They would point out that they stand for abortion, slavery, pornography, gambling and all the vices which have been part of Satan's programs.

Who will tell the Lord that they are in command? Can you imagine Henry Kissinger or David Rockefeller telling the Lord that they are in charge and He must go?

The prophet Malachi was correct to question "Who shall stand?"

THE ULTIMATE PRAYER

One glance at a newspaper today replete with its accounts of murder, rape, terrorism, drug addiction and related in humanism would lead one to believe that the world has gone MAD. In the United States, the best apparent single solution to these problems is to spend more money—a solution that so far, has eluded all the spending efforts of politicians, government agencies and do gooders. The ultimate solution and the one which man will resist at all cost, is to turn to God! In turning to God we must do so in prayer.

But, how do we pray?

Jesus himself gave us the admonition to pray and then taught us how to pray.

The ultimate prayer given by Jesus himself in the Sermon on the Mount (Matt. 6:9) is the Lord's Prayer. We find in this magnificent 66 word prayer all of the important elements which could basically be our set of Golden Rules. First, He mentions the Father in Heaven, God's name, God's Kingdom, and God's will. This is followed by a petition for food, forgiveness, sin via temptation, delivery from the Prince of this world—Satan, and concludes acknowledging the Kingdom, Power and Glory of His Father.

When He gave us this prayer, the Lord charged the multitude not to say repetitive words, but to pray as He taught them. He said "Our Father who art in Heaven...". We should note that He did not say My Father, but Our Father. If therefore, He is our Father, we then must be his children. Here Jesus clearly set the record straight. Because God is our Father in Heaven and we His children on earth, we are clearly heirs to the Grace of God and the Kingdom of God! (Gal. 4:6,7). We therefore occupy a unique relationship - that of a father to his child. The good Father will give the inheritance of his Kingdom to his children, his love, protection, security, guidance, favors, food and clothing; moreover, these gifts are freely given in love by the Father. The Father is also bound by His Love to chasten (Heb. 12:7), guide, lead and protect His children.

As children of God, recipients of His many blessings, we are free to accept or reject the gifts of the Father. Well do we know, how man from time immemorial, has refused the gifts of the Father to follow the uncertain paths of his own weak judgment. We have the power of obtaining all things since the Father in His Love for us is a kind and loving Father—all we need to do is ask (Matt. 7:7).

IN HEAVEN

The Father is in heaven, not here on earth. Since the Father is not of this earth, we need a contact to bridge the gap between heaven and earth and that bridge is Jesus Christ (Jn 3:16). He came to earth, died and is alive today to return soon in full glory as ruler of the Kindgom of God. (Rev.19:11).

HALLOWED BE THY NAME

Why would Christ so early in this prayer stress the importance of His holy name? Clearly, God alone should we worship (Ex. 20:5). We should hold the name of God in reverence and always praise His name.

How can we praise the name of God?

We can praise the name of God by reflecting on the handiwork of His creation. As Jesus said, "Look at the birds of the air" or "Consider the lilies of the field" (Matt 6:26-28). Notice how He turns to the marvelous works of the Father in presenting lasting word images - images that indeed have survived for some 2000 years. These marvelous works of God, the trees, birds, flowers, the grasses of the field are all gifts of God from above (James 1:17). By recognizing these wonders and appreciating its source, we can praise God.

THY KINGDOM COME

The Kingdom of God is mentioned many times by Jesus directly and in parables. Why did Jesus pray for the coming of the Kingdom? He fully realized the imperfect governments controlled by man, replete with sin, graft, greed, corruption and chaos was in no way to be compared to a government ruled by God and characterized by eternal peace and justice. There would be no need for laws, armies or police forces in a Kingdom where Love of God and neighbor is the rule practiced by all (Lk 10:27) freely and in love for God and fellow man. We as Christians need more than ever to pray for the coming of His Kingdom.

THY WILL BE DONE

God's will not our will! How often have we prayed for our will to be done. If we look back on some of the requests we have made of God, we may be surprised to find that we tend to look at the small picture, while God sees the big picture. We would also be pleasantly surprised to find that when God answers our prayers, it is to His greater glory, we receive many times that which we requested - truly our cups run over! We should also remember that God says "NO" and this is indeed an answer, although we are not always prepared for the negative response and do not recognize it as God's answer. In many cases, God answers in His good time. Long after we give up, we may find that He still remembers and then gives to us abundantly. Consider Elizabeth and Zachary. The angel said to Zachary "Your petition has been heard" (Lk 1:13).

By the time Elizabeth had conceived, it is doubtful that she and Zachary was still praying for a child, yet their earlier petition was miraculously answered—God did not forget and the birth of John the Baptist was to the greater glory of God. Since God's will is also done in Heaven, He is therefore ruler of the universe—all things are under His control as indeed it is!

God's will on earth is also done. Consider the birth of Jesus that was promised hundreds of years before its occurrence (Isa, 7:14). The unusual circumstances surrounding His birth and the events preceding it are too numerous to cite. For example, the Birth of John the Baptist, the Annunciation in which God through that forced the birth to occur at Bethlehem instead of in Nazareth, thus fulfilling the prophecy His angel Gabriel intervenes into the events on earth. The occurrence of the census (Mich. 5:2), and the announcement to the shepherds are sufficient examples to show the way in which God's will is done on earth as it is in heaven.

GIVE US THIS DAY

In the Sermon on the Mount, Jesus chided the people for being anxious about material things. He cited the birds of the air—how His heavenly Father feeds them (He still does!!). He also exemplified His power over food in His miraculous extension of the loaves and fishes (Mk 6:41). We can still see His hand today in the abundance of food He provides for us. One need not be reminded how in a single night, a chilling frost can wipe out a whole year's crop. It is His hand that can stay the devastation of the weather, control our food supply and His mercy that provides the abundance of food to feed the earth. More dramatic was the manner in which He fed the Israelites for forty years in the desert (Ex.16: 4,5) and the widow at Seraphta (3 Kings 17:14). How often do we take for granted the gift of our daily bread? Imagine a worldwide season of bad weather- portions of which we are witnessing today in the midwest, Israel and Russia in the year 1972. God can and does control our daily bread (Mk.11:20).

AND FORGIVE US

Jesus pointed to the fact that we are all sinners in His rebuke of those who condemned the woman taken in adultery (Jn 8: 7). No one there could counter this single charge, "Let he who is without sin among you cast the first stone—". We all sin, but have a means for forgiveness by recourse to the Father. He who forgives also reminds us to forgive in kind those who sin against us. If each of us would take this admonition seriously and practice it to the letter, we would have a vehicle for world peace that could transform the world from its present confused, hopeless state to a paradise on earth. Here again we see the tremendous impact of this powerful prayer. The greatest difficulty lies in man's ability to practice forgiveness to others.

AND LEAD US NOT INTO TEMPTATION

We walk a tightrope to salvation! We are constantly buffeted on all sides by numerous daily temptations: lust, greed, envy, anger, hatred, selfishness and materialism. These temptations are not mean distractions, but a concentrated, determined program to keep us from salvation. Ever since Adam and Eve first succumbed to the first temptation, man has been living in a constant deluge of temptation (Gen. 3: 1-5). We are so concerned today with materialism, status, conformity, being relevant and consenting that moral values have been suppressed to an awesome level. We hear a lot today about four letter words and the overworking of the word LOVE. Yet, the three-letter word is the key to our fall and to our salvation. All of man's troubles can be laid to one word, SIN. Sin caused our loss of paradise and sin is the ultimate cause of all of our troubles today, as it has been in the past. Fortunately, we have salvation in the one GOD who will overcome SIN. Jesus through His death convicted the world of sin and God will save us from sin! (Jn 16:8).

DELIVER US FROM EVIL

Here some translations refer to the evil one - the devil - Satan. Jesus wisely included this petition in His prayer. To those who are inclined to scoff at the existence of the devil, note the prominent part he played in the New Testament. Recognizing the impending threat that Jesus posed to his kingdom, Satan intervened early in Jesus' public life. The temptation must have been awesome and one which few, if any, could have successfully resisted. Imagine being promised the wealth of the kingdoms of the earth vs death on the cross -who could turn such a temptation down?

The world is still in the clutches of the devil, but fortunately, he has already been judged (Jn 16:11). We must only await the execution of the sentence promised in Revelation 20:9, only then can true peace exist on the earth. Regardless of how hard we try to achieve peace, we are no match for the devil. Consider the United Nations, an organization dedicated to peace in the world. This body has become a weak tool of the devil in its inability to achieve or enforce peace. It is interesting to note that the U. N. was doomed to failure from its inception in that it slammed the door in the face of the Prince of Peace. If God had been the corner stone of its charter, perhaps that body would not be the weak, sterile organization it is today.

KINGDOM AND POWER

Truly His is the Kingdom, Power and Glory. How fortunate we are to be on the other side of the promise. Consider those who before Christ's time had the promise, but did not see the salvation of Jesus and the revelation of His kingdom to come. Our salvation is now assured - the ransom has been paid. It is only for us to accept this free gift of salvation to inherit the Kingdom of Heaven Rev.21:1).

The constant reminder of His kingdom in this Ultimate Prayer - The Lord's Prayer - should be a hope, comfort and a joy to all who believe in the LORD JESUS CHRIST

YOU WILL NEVER WALK AGAIN

Have you ever witnessed a real miracle? Miracles are recorded in the bible and in many stories over the ages, but to witness one is an unusual experience. The miracle that Carol and I witnessed occurred in Michigan City at the Holy Trinity Ukrainian Orthodox Church beginning on April 2, 1995 when the Icon began to stream myrrh, a miracle that lasted for several months.

The Icon is a crucifix made of olive wood and over a hundred years old. When news of the miracle spread, thousands flocked to the church to witness the phenomenon. After a few weeks, Carol and I drove to Michigan City to see first hand the miracle. And miracle is was! From all the wounds of Christ one could see drops of myrrh slowly running down and gathered in glass bowls. We were so impressed that we returned five times to see this until the stream stopped and the Icon was returned to its place behind the altar.

A few years later Carol and I had a miracle of our own. Carol was diagnosed with follicular thyroid cancer with three tumors on her spine.

This caused a rapid progressive paralysis. After being treated with surgery, radiation and nuclear medicine her prognosis was dismal. She was told that she would be wheel chair bound for the rest of her life.

Then came physical therapy with a wonderful therapist, Mary Pat, who was an angel sent. Carol was determined that with prayer and God's Healing Mercy, she would walk again. Prayers of our friends and our own faith were answered and Carol began to walk again in six months.

Being an active gardener with gorgeous flowerbeds and plantings she dedicated her garden to God as a tribute to His Healing Mercy.

This was indeed our second miracle.

TALES FROM THE BUSINESS WORLD

THOMAS J. MIRANDA

ABUSE!!

*We trained hard...but it seemed that every time we were beginning
to form up into teams, we would be reorganized. I was to learn late
in life that we tend to meet any new situation by reorganizing;
and a wonderful method it can be for creating the illusion of progress,
while producing confusion, inefficiency and demoralization*
- Petronius Arbiter, 210 B.C.

We hear a lot about abuse today. The media is constantly reminding us about child, drug, environmental, spouse and other abuse that unfortunately has become a part of our society. One of the most neglected areas of abuse today is ASSET ABUSE. This is a sinister practice conducted by upper management and encouraged by the gurus of our Business Schools. Here's how it works. During the fifties and sixties, management found that, using the principles of management taught by people like Maslow and others, by treating people fairly they encouraged high morale, a sense of belonging, commitment, reward and praise. The net result was that people felt that they were a part of a team, worked for the common goal and were rewarded for their extra efforts through bonuses, promotions and other recognition of their efforts. With the new philosophy now being taught by the business schools, management has now thrown those sound principles out in favor of worshiping the current bottom line and doing whatever is necessary to show a profit in each quarter. This shortterm goal has become the norm regardless of the long term effects on the business and more importantly with little regard for their most important asset-PEOPLE. Think about it! If a CEO mismanaged an asset, the Board of Directors would make short work of his tenure in that post. Yet today upper management is often guilty of gross mismanagement of one of their most important assets - PEOPLE. In a highly motivated organization, people will work as a team, put in extra hours and apply their creativity to improve the company's competitive position. (If you don't believe this, just look a your company's parking lot at quitting time; or even fifteen minutes before quitting time! In the not too distant past, I can recall seeing the lots full long after the normal quitting time; yet today the lots are quickly emptied at or long before normal closing). Just how much money is a firm losing in man-hours, creativity, enthusiasm and return on assets by poor people management? With the new thinking, using subjective appraisal systems, forced ratings and disregard for people, management is throwing away a valued asset. For example, most firms will seek out the best qualified candidates for a position, generally the top 10 percentile. Yet, in the forced rating systems, performance is rated on and force fitted to a specific curve. This has a negative effect on motivation, teamwork, and enthusiasm and more importantly on the people contribution to the welfare of the firm. Another example, which can be found today in many firms, is the disregard for people performance. There are numerous examples of people who have been outstanding performers, who now, because of the new thinking, are rated as average or below average with subsequent loss of merit bonuses, pay increases and promotions just to satisfy a management goal such as "Managing-to-One" or some other form of Human Resource "Doublespeak". Unfortunately, managers who mistreat this most important asset are frequently hailed by Business Publications and cited as "CEO of the Year." How can management be so foolish? Are they aware of this loss of assets; don't they care or is it both? While American management continues on this destructive course of worshiping the short-term bottom line, while neglecting their people, the foreign competition will beat them again and again.

ASSET ABUSE MUST BE STOPPED...NOW!!

Thomas J. Miranda   TECHNICAL EDITOR

DIPHENOLIC ACID

When Grandpa Bigdog graduated from Notre Dame, he got a job at the O'Brien Corporation as Director of Research. My task was to develop new technology for O'Brien.

Actually GBD was really lost and had no real idea what to do. So one thing I did was to scan the literature for any possible ideas. Well, one day I found an ad placed by S. C. Johnson regarding a new venture in organic chemicals. They were offering diphenolic acid as an intermediate for making polymers.

So GBD answered the ad and received some literature and samples. Later I was surprised to receive a phone call from S. C. Johnson wanting to meet with me at O'Brien to discuss ideas and possible uses.

So on the appointed day here came the Vice President of Marketing and son-in-law of the Johnson family and Dr. Howard C. W—a consultant who worked for S. C. Johnson and reported directly to the Vice President.

Well, Dr. W—looked like a used car salesman and was smoking a huge cigar and blowing smoke all over. (Actually, he had a high vapor pressure, as we shall see later). All in all he was a huge foghorn.

Dr. W—suggested that he bring a team from Racine to review what they had done to date. So I invited John C. Lauder, who was in charge of can coatings for O'Brien and a number of others.

When W—mentioned can coatings, Lauder, who was a real operator quickly shoved GBD aside and took over. Johnson chemists had made a can coating using DPA and were eager to try it on the inner liner of beer cans...coatings we sold to Continental Can.

Lauder saw a real chance to be a hero and made arrangements for a trial run in our laboratory. So the Johnson people flew down in a propeller driven airplane with their new coating and got there near noontime. They quickly applied the varnish to the roll coating machine and started the coater. Alas, the coating began to gel and the test was scrapped.

So the Johnson people got back on their plane and headed back to Racine. The next week they had a new formulation and this time they flew down on a jet and made a successful run on the coater, coating several sheets of beer can blanks.

But unfortunately as we stood around the lab, the varnish gelled. So off to the conference room they went to discuss the problem. This time GBD was invited to attend the meeting.

As everyone was trying to figure out why the varnish was unstable, GBD pointed out that they had neglected the fact that DPA is trifunctional and prone to cause gellation. I further suggested that they use the methyl ester, which is difunctional, and then prepare the varnish.

"This is a serious meeting and we have no time for foolish tales", said Lauder. "If you can't make a contribution, then you can leave".

So GBD went back to the lab and prepared a varnish using the methyl ester and it did not gel. GBD filed a patent and the patent examiner divided the application into two patents.

Meanwhile, a chemist from Johnson called me at home one night to ask me to check into Dr. W—. I wrote to Miami University only to find out that he never received a Ph. D there. When I sent the letter to the Johnson chemist, he was fired.

But these clowns are like corks...they never sink. After laying low for a while he was hired by a Texas paint company and continued his scam as Dr. W—. He was still ten minutes ahead of the posse.

S. C. Johnson finally sold the business to the Japanese who were successful in marketing the amide of DPA for adhesive applications.

Watch out for foghorns!!

131

ONE O'CLOCK SURPRISE

The Dexter Corporation, Windsor Locks, CT is one of the largest producers of paper used in the teabag business. One of their subsidiaries, the Midland Division has a facility on the western shore of Lake Michigan in Waukegan, Illinois.

Midland is noted for their high performance coatings used for power plant stacks, high heat applications and unique silicone bearing materials for the coatings industry.

On the second floor of this facility there is a large conference room overlooking the lake. This is where many company meetings are held with the fringe benefit being the great view.

One day a Technical Representative called on the Research Director and asked him if he could arrange a meeting with the higher ups to present their line of products. He insisted that the meeting be attended by the Division President and as many important people as possible.

Accordingly, a meeting was set up for 1:00 p.m. on a given day. After the Research Director phoned the Technical Rep to confirm the date and time, the Technical Rep said, "Have I got a surprise for you."

On the appointed day the Research Director alerted the important people and moved up to the conference room. By 12:30 the Technical Rep had not yet arrived and the Research Director became a bit concerned. Soon the important people began to show signs of uneasiness as they stared out over the lake.

Suddenly, a seaplane swooped down and landed in the lake in full view.

It was the salesman! This was his big surprise!

As the plane began to taxi toward the conference room it hit a floating log and began to sink. They quickly called the Coast Guard to rescue the surprise.

I don't know if he ever got to give his presentation that day.

ANECTDOTES FROM THE COATINGS WORLD

In the coatings industry as well as other industries, everyday operations can sometimes lead to humorous situations. These may not be funny at the time, are sometimes embarrassing and even costly. However, they do occur and valuable lessons can be gleaned from these situations.

Listed below are several anecdotes which this author has had personal experience or known of them through reliable sources.

THE LUNATICS

One of the major milestones in the Coatings Industry was the development of electrocoating. Credit for this great discovery must be assigned to Dr. George E.F. Brewer, a Staff Scientist at the Ford Motor Company. The preferred priming method for industrial processes was flow coating. In this process the paint is pumped and sprayed over the car body. The excess paint was recirculated. Following this, the parts were moved into a solvent chamber to level the film. This was a very hazardous process as demonstrated at a General Motors transmission plant at Wixom, Michigan that was leveled by fire when a welder's torch near the vapor chamber sparked the fire.

Another disadvantage of flow coating was that in closed structures, such as the interior of door panels or rocker panels, the vapor washed the deposited paint away. This explains why so many corrosion problems occurred in automobiles.

Dr. Brewer was searching for a better process and turned to the latex industry and borrowed a process of electrophoresis to solve his problem. To make latex gloves and condoms, latex dispersions are electrophoretically deposited on molds. George felt that this technology could be used to replace flow coating and being water dispersible, a much safer process.

His early attempts to produce an effective coating were not successful until he got a boost from Alan Gilchrist of the Glidden Company who prepared maleic anhydride modified linseed oil adducts that were water dispersible from which adequate primers could be formulated.

Dr. Brewer's manager was Gilbert Burnside who was a tough, hard driving engineer and together they forged ahead on the project. To gain support from Ford's upper management, George arranged a meeting with a Ford executive to discuss his plan. He and Burnside explained to the executive how they proposed to build a 50,000 gallon tank, fill it with paint,

133

dip the whole car into the tank, apply 500 volts d.c. to the car body and "plate" the car with primer. The executive listened politely, then as this impressive duo left his office, he turned to his secretary and said:

"NOT ONE DIME FOR THOSE TWO LUNATICS".

Today, electrocoating is applied all over the world.

FISHEYES

One of the banes of resin production is the formation of foam. For example, when preparing alkyds, varnishes or urea or melamine formaldehyde resins, there is a tendency to develop foam. This is especially true near the end of a reaction, when the viscosity increases. A run away foam can carry the contents of the reactor right up the condenser and spew it over the plant area.

To stop a rising foam, a number of antifoam additives have been used with varying success. For example, pine oil and triphenyl phosphate are effective antifoam agents.

A major breakthrough occurred in the foam problem when silicone technology was developed. Low molecular weight silicones were found to be very effective in breaking foams. However, a little went a long way and too much could lead to cratering or fisheyes in finished films.

The O'Brien Corporation supplied automotive finishes to the Studebaker Corporation in the fifties. One day the production line was shut down due to cratering on the topcoats of Studebaker automobiles. This caused much concern and launched a campaign of finger pointing up and down the process chain. Eventually, this was traced to a melamine-formaldehyde product made by American Cyanamid. Apparently, AntiFoam A® had just been introduced to their manufacturing process and operators were more interested in controlling foam than in the consequences of on line performance of the finished product.

MORE FISHEYES

The St. Joseph, Michigan plant of the Whirlpool Corporation produced washing machines. These units were flow coat primed and top coated with an acrylic finish. The suppliers were reliable and had good track records of finish performance on production lines.

As with all well run operations, there are some anomalies that occur from time to time and this plant was no exception. One day, out of the blue, washer cabinets began to form fisheyes. This caused great concern for all and immediate action was taken to identify the source of the contamination.

Problems of this type involve a number of steps that finish engineers follow to isolate potential causes. Some of these include metal treatment operations, rinsing, spray equipment and a review of the formulations by the suppliers. After many blind trails, the engineers began to notice that the problem appeared to strike on a Thursday and tapered off as the week went on until cratering stopped.

After another day of futile searching, the supplier and Whirlpool people took a break and went to the cafeteria. As they were sitting there discussing the problem, someone noticed that the fast food vendor was servicing the dispensing machines and was busy spraying the mechanism inside the vending machines. On closer examination it was noted that the spray was loaded with silicone and the air intake of the spray booth was located in the cafeteria. So, all the chemistry, analyses and other efforts were reduced to a matter of keen observation by a competent technical serviceman.

THE ELECTROCOAT TANK

During a hot summer day, Joe DeVittorio of Sherwin-Williams was making a call at a customer's electrocoat facility. Joe was always impeccably dressed. In fact, if you saw him on any business day you would think that he was on his way to have his picture taken.

On this particular day the Sherwin-Williams people had been working on some problems with the customer's tank and Joe was there to provide expertise and support. Nearing mid afternoon Joe was required to leave to catch a plane back to Chicago and decided to take one last walk around the electrocoat tank. As he walked around the tank, he fell into the tank and was quickly fished out.

Faced with a time constraint and the fact that he had no other clothes, the customer rinsed his suit with water and ran it through the paint oven for a quick dry. (Anodic electrocoating tanks were neutralized with amines that over time can produce some foul odors like that of rotting fish.) Joe quickly dressed with his suit now shrunk and extremely wrinkled and headed for the airport.

One familiar with amine odor contamination can just imagine what that plane ride home did for Joe and for the unfortunate passengers who had to sit near him.

THE INTERVIEW

Dr. Marco Wismer is a former vice president of PPG Industries. Marco received his technical training in Switzerland prior to coming to the United States. He, along with Joe Bosso, is credited with the invention of cationic electrocoating, a major leapfrog technology for the coatings industry.

When Dr. Wismer first came to America, he began interviewing for a job. One of his interviews was with the DuPont Company in Wilmington, Delaware. Marco took a train to Wilmington and checked into the local YMCA for the night. (It is customary in European hotels to place ones shoes in the hallway at night so the floor attendant can polish the guest's shoes).

Upon retiring for the night, Marco placed his shoes in the hallway. The next morning there were no shoes to be found. So Marco went to his interview at Dupont dressed in a business suit and wearing tennis shoes.

POMP AND CIRCUMSTANCE

Sometimes, even the most pompous event can lose its esteem with a single word or phrase. Here is an example:

The J. J. Mattiello Lecture Award is the highest award presented to recognize people who have made significant accomplishments. This coveted award is presented annually at the Federation of Societies for Coatings Technology Convention where the Mattiello Lecture is delivered by the honored individual. The lecture is well attended and highly publicized.

In 1973 Dr. George E. F. Brewer was the Mattiello Awardee. The lecture was presented in the Grand Ballroom of the Conrad Hilton Hotel in Chicago and his topic was electrocoating. I was particularly interested in the subject and wanted to hear George, since he and I used to exchange ideas on water soluble polymers.

The Chairman of the Mattiello Committee introduces the speaker and for some reason, I timed the introductory remarks, which went on for a full seven minutes. One could not be unimpressed with the impeccable background and expertise of this famous scientist and I was quite awestruck.

George began his talk with a description of the corrosion problems inherent in the automobile in general and with the rocker panel in particular. He then began to speak of the rocker panel in his heavy Hungarian accent. He described the rocker panel as a large welded box fourrrteen feet long. "How do you paint the son of a beech?"

THE DRYER DRUM PROBLEM

Many years ago, Norge built a large dryer plant in Fort Smith, Arkansas. The paint supplier was PPG Industries, which at that time was known as Pittsburgh Plate Glass Company.

The operation operated smoothly for some time until the "fisheye" problem emerged. It appeared that at certain times the fisheyes would appear and cause numerous rejects.

The usual problem solution tasks were then brought into play, such as blaming the paint supplier, who in turn blamed the metal treatment people etc. PPG 's industrial products were well supported by field technical service people with backup all the way to their Springdale, PA R&D facility. The first thing PPG did was to check out the formulation, then modify the coating with alternate anti-cratering agents, test the coating in their laboratories then bring the new formulation to Fort Smith. With each new formulation the performance was acceptable, but the fisheyes would occur, requiring another trip back to the laboratory.

After some time, the cost of servicing this account had grown considerably and PPG management agreed that they could not continue to supply this customer in a cost effective manner. So, they made a final formulation change and took a high ranking official along with the technical service group to discuss the problem at Norge. They told Norge management that this was their last try and they planned to pull out if the problem was not resolved that day.

The final formulation was introduced into the system and ran very well. PPG people remained at the plant long into the night, when shortly after midnight the fisheyes began to appear. PPG people were completely frustrated. One of their technical service men was Erwin Kapalko, who was an accomplished coatings specialist and excellent troubleshooter. He began to walk through the plant to determine if he could spot some causal agent. As he was walking through the far reaches of the plant he heard some women shrieking and laughing. When he reached the spot, he noted that these women were removing dryer drum shells from the conveyer line. Inside some of these drums were condoms thrown in from the front of the line by some smart aleck to get a reaction from the women. The silicone on the condoms was contaminating the product line.

So all the technical effort to resolve this problem was of little value, but the trained eye of a real professional solved a major problem by his keen observation. (I wonder if they fired the guy?)

THE NECKTIE

After World War II many of the technical developments of the Manhattan Project found their way into consumer products. One such product application was to the wringer washing machine. This product was responsible for may home accidents as children would have their limbs caught in the rollers or women would have their loose clothing become entangled in the rollers. There were many safety devices designed to disconnect the rollers and these features were important in selling wringer washers to the public.

Whirlpool engineers found that torque sensor technology could be applied to this problem and designed a washing machine that could be reversed by simply pulling back on material being fed into the rollers. This was a major breakthrough and one that would have tremendous marketing appeal.

As with most firms there are many 'dog and pony' shows to review the latest developments for upper management. So, the Laundry Engineering Group put on a show to demonstrate this latest breakthrough, which was very well received by the hierarchy.

Since Sears Roebuck is a major customer of Whirlpool it was important that their buyers and executives see this 'dog and pony' show and a meeting was scheduled accordingly. Prior to the meeting, the Director of Engineering queried the engineers to assure that nothing would go wrong. To demonstrate the effect of this new safety device wet Turkish towels were fed into the rollers and upon pulling back, the rollers automatically reversed direction.

The Engineering Director was still skeptical so an engineer put his necktie into the rollers and had him pull back. Upon pulling back, the rollers reversed much to the amazement of the Engineering Director. Everything was now set for the big day. After wining and dining the Sears executives on the previous evening, the Laundry Engineers were eager to demonstrate their masterpiece.

After a discussion of the engineering aspects of the invention, they adjourned to the laboratory to demonstrate the wringer washer. Many Turkish towels were run in and out of the wringer with great success. Finally, a Whirlpool executive took the tie of a Sears executive and fed it into the wringer and guess what happened? The sensor failed and the washer began to strangle the hapless man until the plug was pulled and his tie cut with a scissors.

So much for dog and pony shows.

LAWRENCE WELK ORCHESTRA

When Grandpa Bigdog was working at Whirlpool he had to attend a lot of National Meetings. Some of these include the American Chemical Society and Federation of Societies for Coatings Technology and others. GBD was the Technical Editor for the Journal of Coatings Technology and attended all of the Annual Conventions. One year the convention was being held in Los Angeles where GBD presented a paper at the Technical Sessions.

Aunt Caroline was studying Clarinet at that time and really did well on t he instrument. She won first place at the music contests and played in the school band.

Well GBD is a real fan of the Lawrence Welk Orchestra and listens to their TV show at every opportunity.

At this convention the Federation held a banquet and this was a very lavish affair and on this occasion they had hired the Lawrence Welk Orchestra (without Lawrence Welk) under the direction of Myron Florin.

So that evening GBD went to the dinner and sat around to hear the Orchestra and that was a delightful evening. One of the stars was Henry Questa, the clarinet player who is a real talent. During the break, GBD introduced himself to Henry and bought him a drink. During our conversation I asked him if he could give GBD an autograph for Aunt Caroline. This he did not do, but told me instead that they were issuing a new album shortly and that he would send her a copy later.

I also had to opportunity to ask him about the people in the organization and he was very complimentary about Mr. Welk and all the performers. He mentioned that Mr. Welk demanded the best behavior of his stars, on and off the stage. In other words, what you saw is what you got.

He also mentioned how well Mr. Welk treated him and all the members of that musical family.

Well, about six weeks later, an album signed by Mr Questa arrived in the mail for Aunt Caroline and she was thrilled. I also told her what a great talent and fine gentleman Henry Questa is.

JINX

One of the activities Grandpa Bigdog engaged in while at Whirlpool was travel. Because of the nature of our work, we were required to visit a number of companies or universities to explore technology or to discuss existing projects.

When Bob Plante started the Materials and Processing Department at Whirlpool, he and GBD used to travel to Whirlpool Divisions and to the Research Centers of a variety of companies.

A peculiar effect while traveling with Bob was that we seemed to encounter a lot of difficulty on our trips. For example, Bob took a number of us to visit the research center of Caterpillar in Peoria, Illinois. It was a rainy day and by the time we got near LaPorte the windshield washer failed and we had to stop at a service station to get a repair.

On another visit Bob and I were on our way to visit Glidden in Cleveland, Ohio. This was to be a high power meeting and the Director of Research and his staff were waiting to take us to an exclusive club for dinner. Well, we got to South Bend and aboard our plane when the pilot announced that due to controller slowdown we would not be able to take off.

Well, we sat on the plane for two hours. When we finally got to Cleveland it was past 8:00 pm and the Glidden people went home leaving us with the salesman who took us to a late dinner.

One day GBD was trying to figure who was the Jonah in Whirlpool who was causing us problems like this. I soon found out.

One day Bill Hill an engineer in the Manufacturing Research Group wanted to visit our St. Paul plant and asked GBD if he could accompany him, since Bill was not familiar with anyone at the plant.

GBD warned Bill that traveling with me could be hazard because every time I went somewhere with Bob Plante we encountered trouble.

Well we went to St. Paul with no trouble, but on the way back, Northwest had oversold the flight so Bill had to sit in First Class where he was treated royally. So the next day he told me that I was not the jinx and he had proof of that.

A few weeks later Bill told me a story. He and Bob were on a trip to Grand Rapids to a 1:30 meeting and drove Bill's Mercedes diesel. Bob was very interested in Bill's car and kept asking him questions about the car.

Finally Bill asked Bob if he would like to drive the car. Bob eagerly accepted Bill's offer and when they reached the next stoplight they switched places. When the light changed Bob stalled the engine and the car would not start. They had to call a tow truck and missed their meeting.

RETIRED

Recently, a friend of mine retired from Whirlpool after 34 years with the firm. He had done many good things for the welfare of the company and was an excellent contributor in Brainstorming sessions.

At his retirement coffee, I thought that this would be a good time for some of the vice presidents of the firm to come over and give him some recognition for his efforts. As it turned out, not one showed up and the Vice President of Research and Engineering didn't attend.

I thought that this was unusual and wondered about this in view of the imminent retirement that I would be facing a few months hence. As it happened, the Vice Presidents were all away at conferences learning how to improve the morale of their subordinates. They could have saved a lot of money by simply walking across the commons and shaking this man's hand.

When my own retirement party arrived, there were also no vice presidents there either. Then I realized that what really counted were those people who were there. **They were the real important people!!**

This is a good lesson for us. Jesus pointed this out in a number of his teachings to his followers. He noted how people were seeking the first places at a wedding feast and were later told to take a lower seat, since one more important than they had arrived.

We tend to look at people from their station in life rather than deeper into the real person.

THE ROLE OF A TEACHER IN SHAPING THE FUTURE OF AN INDIVIDUAL

Dr. Thomas J. Miranda
WHIRLPOOL CORPORATION

(Speech presented to the Detroit Society for Coatings
Technology Education Night, October 22, 1985)

Thank you for the honor of being chosen to speak to you tonight on the occasion of your annual Education Night. Members of the Detroit Society, I congratulate you for the effort you are making to bring Coatings Technology awareness to the Educational Community. Members of the teaching profession, you are making a valuable contribution to the Coatings Industry, and to your students, by your presence here and it is good to see so many of you here.

141

Tonight, I would like to take a few moments to talk to you about the role of teachers in shaping the lives of their students. Perhaps a good way to do this is to think in terms of catalysts, as people action may be described in terms of catalytic activity, that is a little goes a long way.

We probably all remember the oxygen experiment in high school or college chemistry where we heat a small amount of $KClO_3$ to drive off oxygen that is collected over water. As I remember the experiment, continuous heating yields very little oxygen, but if a trace of manganese dioxide is added, copious amounts of oxygen are liberated. Following the lab book instructions, if we filtered and weighed the residue, we found the manganese dioxide was unreacted. This experiment clearly demonstrates the effect of a catalyst. By definition then, a catalyst is a substance that greatly increases the reaction rate, but does not enter into the reaction.

People too, function as catalysts. Consider the people responsible for setting up this meeting; a few people who impact many. Let me mention a few examples of people who have made significant contributions to the Coatings Industry as examples of what I would consider people catalysts.

MICROVOIDS

One of the real giants in the Coatings Industry was the late Dr. Howard L. Gerhart. He had a strong committment to research and education and his influence is still with us today. His curiosity of natural phenomena led to the discovery of the impact of microvoids in producing hiding. He had once observed a white petunia and wondered why it was white; though there was not one ounce of TiO_2 in the flower. As a result, he set out to find the reason; which resulted in the practical application of microvoids in paints and plastics today.

ELECTRODEPOSITION

Another giant in the coating industry is Dr. George Brewer, of the Detroit Society. While at the Ford Motor Company, he perceived the need to develop improved corrosion resistance in automotive coatings. He foresaw the potential of using electrodeposition as a means of reaching recessed areas in auto bodies and thereby improving corrosion resistance. What is more significant is his persistance in the face of many obstacles to see his concept through to a successful implementation.

I am told of a story about George and his manager who were trying to obtain support for his project in the early stages of development. They reviewed the proposal with a higher level management officer who listened politely. After George left his office, the officer turned to his secretary and said:

"NOT ONE DIME FOR THOSE TWO LUNATICS!!"

Dr. Brewer's invention is practiced today around the world on appliances, automobiles and general metal finishing!!

INFRARED BOOKLET

Another example of people catalysts is Wallace H. Brown, of DeSoto, Inc. Many years ago, when infrared analysis was new to the coatings industry, he and a group of Chicago Society members wrote a small booklet on Infrared Spectroscopy that swept the industry and became one of the most popular books published by the Federation of Societies for Coatings Technology. This book was subsequently revised twice and today is a widely used standard reference in analytical laboratories around the world—an 896 page book containing over 1,400 spectra and more than 1,500 references.

PAINT/COATINGS DICTIONARY

Another real contributor is Stanley Le Sota of the Rohm and Haas Company. He chaired a committee of dedicated people and labored for 13 years to finally publish the dictionary containing 5,500 entries and an elaborate appendix of references and source material. This represented over 5,000 hours of volunteer effort and required a real catalyst to see it to completion.

FEDERATION SERIES

Another group of people catalysts is the Publications Committee of the Federation of Societies for Coatings Technology. These individuals volunteer many hours of their personal time to review manuscripts for the Journal of Coatings Technology that make that Journal the definitive journal in the field. A significant accomplishment is the Federation Booklets on Coatings Technology. These 27 Booklets have been a vital educational tool in universities, seminars, coatings courses and in coatings laboratories to teach new entrants in the field, as well as, to serve experienced technologists. Unfortunately, these booklets are out of date but fortunately, Dr. Darlene Brezinski of DeSoto, Inc. and I have undertaken the task of updating, rewriting and formatting a new series of monographs which should begin publication in the coming year. These monographs should be a valued resource for the Coatings Industry.

ROLE OF A TEACHER IN SHAPING THE FUTURE OF AN INDIVIDUAL

I would like to take a few moments now, to discuss the role of teachers in shaping the lives of their students.

One of my early goals in life was to be a High School Science Teacher. This was short lived since I flunked out of high school in my first year. When I returned, I struggled along with C and D grades until I began my Junior year. The History teacher, who was also the Chemistry teacher, challenged us that if we studied in a manner that he would propose, he assured us that our grades would improve in the next grading period. I took up the challenge which Mr. Mieschke dropped and when the report cards came, I received B grades for the first time since the third grade. In my senior year, I received straight A grades.

Another teacher who had an influence in my life was the Algebra Teacher. He was also the HiY director for our club. At our last meeting, he announced that he had gifts for the graduating seniors and proudly passed them out. When I unwrapped my gift I found out that it was not a gift at all—it was a NEW TESTAMENT. I was expecting a real gift like a pen or pocketknife. He then asked if we would like to have it autographed, which I did. I took the 'gift' home and dropped it into a dresser drawer.

After graduation, I became a motion picture projectionist, a lonely job, and one night while looking for reading material to pass away the hours, I took the New Testament to work. After wading through the begats in Matthew, I finally came to the Sermon on the Mount. It was then that I realized what a **TREASURE** this man had given me. I then turned back to the inscription which read:

TO: Tom Miranda
FROM: C. P. Klassen
Psa. 32:8

Now Psalm 32:8 reads, *"I will instruct thee and teach thee in the way that thou shall go; I will guide thee with mine eye"*

The next teacher who influenced my life was after I had graduated from college. Dr. Albert Castro was a Visiting Professor at Johns Hopkins University while I was in the army and Carol and I visited his family on a

Sunday afternoon. He and Carol were huddled in serious conversation for a good part of the day and upon returning home, Carol pointed a finger at me and said: "You have one month to find a graduate school. Al and I were discussing your future and he indicated that you must get a Ph.D." So, off we went to Notre Dame-a decision I never regretted.

Later on, I encountered another teacher, Professor John Peck, who also influenced my life. As with Dr. Castro, he too had a co- conspirator; my son Mike who was an accounting student at IUSB. One night Mike announced that Dr. Peck was coming over to talk about the MBA program. I listened politely then forgot about it. During dinner, one evening a bit later, Mike handed me some computer cards and told me that he had enrolled me at IUSB and I was starting that night with Statistics and Systems Analysis.

About that time I was working on Flame Retardant plastics and having a very difficult time trying to develop a systems approach to the problem. In the first two weeks of the course, Dr. Nasta explained his method of solving problems using his Eleven Point procedure. Within a few weeks, I put a program together and gave a presentation to Monsanto Research. The Research Director expressed amazement at the depth and scope which I had developed, thanks to Dr. Nasta. I still use his method.

I hope that some day, as a teacher, I can repay the great favors these teachers did for me. In a small way perhaps, I may have begun. Last October, I received the J.J. Mattiello Memorial Lecture Award in Chicago. As I was standing in the Grand Ballroom of the Conrad Hilton, prior to giving my lecture, a young man approached me and told me that he was completing his Ph.D at North Dakota State in Polymer Chemistry. He went on to point out that the reason he selected Polymer Chemistry was that he had heard a lecture I gave on the subject at IUSB several years ago and was so impressed, that he decided to make that his career.

So to those teachers who helped me I am deeply grateful, and to the teachers here tonight I would remind you that somewhere, sometime, you too may be the catalyst that sparks the **creativity, drive** and **enthusiasm** in someone and that **TREASURE** will be with them all their lives.

PROBLEM SOLVING
Dr. M. Nasta

1. DESCRIPTION OF THE PROBLEM

2. INFORMATION AVAILABLE

3. INFORMATION REQUIREMENTS

4. CRITERIA TO EVALUATE THE ALTERNATIVES

5. OBJECTIVE(S)

6. ALTERNATIVES OR DECISION VARIABLES

7. ASSUMPTIONS

8. CONSTRAINTS OR RESTRICTIONS

9. OTHER RELATED SYSTEMS

10. ANALYSIS AND EVALUATION (OR COMPARISONS)
OF VARIOUS ALTERNATIVES

11. BEST ALTERNATIVE(S)

THE DESK TOP

T. F. Washburn Company was a regional paint manufacturer in Chicago, which formulates and sells Trade Sales paint in the area. In order to increase sales, they try to encourage area distributors to carry their line of paint, which is competitive with other area manufacturers.

One particular distributor came down pretty hard on Washburn countering that they could buy essentially the same paint from Jewel, Standard T or Valspar. The president of the company told the Washburn people to come back only when they had something unique and they would consider selling their paint.

Meanwhile, in Minneapolis General Mills had developed some new chemistry based on fatty amines, that is products derived from the reaction of fatty acids and polyamines. These resins were called "Polyamide resins". When reacted with epoxy resins, they could form a two component coating system with outstanding properties. (see the Toilet Seat problem)

Polyamides could also be used to make alkyd resins. An unusual property of polyamide alkyds was that they could be formulated into a thixotropic paint. The paint simply did not flow and the can could be turned upside down and no paint would pour out. However, when a brush is inserted into the paint, the paint could be applied to a surface without dripping or spattering.

In order to develop a market for this, General Mills made an agreement with Washburn to formulate a line of alkyd paints which could be advertised as non-drip, non-spattering paint.

THIS WOULD BE A MARKET SENSATION!!!

Armed with this potent new marketing tool, the Washburn people sought and obtained an appointment with the president of the distribution company for 11:00 a.m. on next Tuesday.

THEY HAD A REAL SURPRISE FOR HIM!!

On the appointed day, the Washburn people entered the president's office with a quart of their new thixotropic paint. But, instead of demonstrating the paint, the company president wanted to show off his new desk. He had just spent a fortune on an imported hand carved desk and everyone oohed and aahed over this beautiful desk until noon.

It was now lunchtime so the company president suggested they delay the demo until after lunch. He suggested he drive his big Cadillac so they all piled in and put the paint can on the rear shelf to be warmed in the sun during a lengthy lunch.

After lunch they returned to the president's office and made their pitch. Here was something a paint that won't drip or spatter.

The Washburn salesman proceeded to open the can of paint and tipped it upside down. The paint came rushing out of the can all over the imported desk...ruining the top of the desk.

Washburn did not make a sale, but they did get the opportunity to pay for refinishing the ruined desk.

Polyamides anyone?

THE TOILET SEAT AFFAIR

In the early sixties, epoxy resins were making a big splash in the coatings industry. They were being heralded for pipe coatings because of their superior corrosion and abrasion resistance.

Another big event that revolutionized the coatings industry was the introduction into trade sales applications of a two-component epoxy resin system that had remarkable properties. This system consisted of a component of EPON 1001® and a Versamid® polyamide resin sold by General Mills. This remarkable coating had a high gloss, excellent adhesion, chemical, and water resistance. Coatings made from this system made excellent swimming pool liners and many pool owners had the coating applied to their pools. Other applications followed.

The O'Brien Corporation marketed a version of this and called it MiraPlate® and its marketing director began to find as many applications as possible. One application evolved in which it was determined that MiraPlate® was great for refurbishing toilet seats. The procedure was to mix component A the epoxy fraction, with component B the polyamide fraction, allow it to sit for one hour then apply. It took about 12 hours for cure.

A certain homeowner bought some MiraPlate® and applied it to the seat in his home. That evening he and his wife attended a function and hired a baby sitter, but forgot to inform the baby sitter of the new breakthrough in the bathroom. Sometime during the evening, after putting the children to bed the baby sitter required a visit to the MiraPlate® coated toilet seat. But, as the babysitter tried to stand up, the excellent adhesive properties of the coating prevented her from rising...she was fixed to the seat.

She was finally able to rouse one of the children, who called the fire department. When they arrived, they too were not up to the adhesive properties of the epoxy coating. They in turn called a physician. When the physician arrived and saw the situation, he burst out laughing so hard he fell into the tub and broke his jaw. The firemen then tried solvents to no avail.

Finally, two burly firemen grabbed the poor girl by the arms and jerked her off the seat along with a layer of epoxy paint.

NEXT WEEK
THOMAS J. MIRANDA

In the industrial world there are many activities that go on. Many of these are serious and require talented people to do their jobs at the best of their abilities. However, in the process, even the talented can foul up and do foolish or embarrassing things.

When Grandpa Bigdog was Director of Research at the O'Brien Corporation, he was involved in a number of different activities. These included the development of emulsion polymers for making wall paint; polymers for can coatings and thermosetting acrylics. In addition, he had a major effort to develop water dispersible polymers that could be used to make semi-gloss enamels. This was a key project requiring a considerable effort.

GBD had invented a novel thermosetting acrylic resin based on oxazoline chemistry and had received two patents on the invention. GBD was invited to present a paper on this at the American Chemical Society's meeting in Pittsburgh in April.

While this was going on Dr. William Burlant at Ford Motor Company developed an exciting new technology. Radiation curing of paint, was a hot topic in the industrial coating field. Well, GBD had some experience in radiation chemistry so he began to synthesize some prepolymers, which were curable by electron beam or ultraviolet radiation.

The O'Brien Corporation started a new division Radiation Polymer Corporation in Plainfield, Illinois and GBD provided the chemistry for that project.

Unfortunately the people involved in RPC were ten minutes ahead of the posse and were difficult to work with.

One day the head of RPC came to O'Brien and told us that there was going to be a symposium on Radiation Curing at the Pittsburgh and insisted that I attend.

Well, GBD had already been scheduled to go on Wednesday since the meeting started then and his paper was to be presented on Friday afternoon. Well the RPC man insisted I go on Monday, so GBD changed his flight and left on Monday.

It was a warm April day so GBD took a light raincoat and headed off for the airport.

Well, as the plane was coming in for a landing the stewardess came flying up the aisle reporting a fire in the rear galley. The plane landed safely, then GBD couldn't find a cab, but took a bus into Pittsburgh to the William Penn hotel.

At the front of the hotel, was a work crew unloading jackhammers to dig up the streetcar tracks. This was o.k. GBD thought since he would be on a high floor...no luck, GBD was on the fifth floor overlooking the street and had to listen to the jackhammers all night long.

GBD then went to dinner and the host placed him facing a pillar and I got my suit coat sleeve in the sour cream of my baked potato. What else can go wrong?

Well the weather changed to a real cold day. GBD took a shower and got into bed and began to look at the program schedule for the meeting...**OH, NO!!!**

The meeting is <u>next</u> week!!

ABOUT THE AUTHOR

The author was born on a sugar plantation, Ewa Mill, Oahu and grew up in Honolulu and lived there until almost a year after the Pearl Harbor bombing that he witnessed. He moved to California, graduated from San Jose State College, taught there for one year, served in the Army Chemical Corps, then received a PhD from Notre Dame University in Organic Chemistry.

His business experiences include Director of Research for the O'Brien Corporation, Staff Scientist at Whirlpool Corporation and Adjunct Professor at Indiana University South Bend. He also served as Technical Editor for the Federation of Societies for Coatings Technology's Journal of Coatings Technology for twenty years and Editor of the Monograph Series on Coatings Technology.

He received a number of local and National Awards for Outstanding Scientific Accomplishment and the Distinguished Business Alumnus Award from the Business School of Indiana University South Bend from which he received the MSBA degree.

He has published over 50 papers, book chapters and is the author of 13 United States Patents.

CPSIA information can be obtained at www.ICGtesting.com
Printed in the USA
LVOW10*0037240115

424141LV00002B/38/P